# STYLE&YOU

EVERY WOMAN'S GUIDE TO TOTAL STYLE

BY

C L A R E   R E V E L L I

P O C K E T   B O O K S

Illustrated by Dennis and David Redmond

ALSO AVAILABLE BY CLARE REVELLI...

COLOR AND YOU (book) . . . A Guide to Discovering Your Best Wardrobe Colors from Pocket Books

COLOR AND YOU (video) . . . Color and Style Tips on Makeup, Haircolor, Accessories, Wardrobe from Simon & Schuster/Paramount Video

MAKING NEWS (newsletter) . . . Clare Revelli on Color, Style and You! from Revelli Design Corporation

For additional information please refer to page 94 or write:

REVELLI
1850 Union Street, San Francisco, CA 94123
(415) 673-6313

Every effort has been made to provide accurate color throughout this book. However, due to certain limitations in four-color printing, some discrepancies may occur. Therefore, color demonstrated in this book should be used only as a guideline.

Another Original publication of POCKET BOOKS

POCKET

POCKET BOOKS, a division of Simon & Schuster, Inc.
1230 Avenue of the Americas, New York, N.Y. 10020

Copyright © 1989 by Clare Revelli

Design & Illustrations by D. Redmond Design

First Pocket Books trade paperback printing March 1989
ISBN: 0-671-67682-2

10 9 8 7 6 5 4 3 2 1

Printed in Spain

# ACKNOWLEDGMENTS

With special appreciation to Dennis and David Redmond for their enthusiasm, dedication, and talented art work . . . to Joan and Eleanor of WIT for their counsel, intellect and remarkable energy . . . to Boris Mlawer for his expertise and attention to detail . . . to John Groton for his years of support and super staff . . . to Claire Zion for her editorial acumen and guidance . . . to Nora Hampton for teaching and inspiring me to write . . . to Lenore Maionchi for her friendship and long hours at work . . . to Florence Revelli for her great mother/style . . . to Grant August Schieldt for his patience, love and cooking dinner . . . and to Sophia for her challenging nature!

## DEDICATION

This book is dedicated to every individual
who aspires to develop her own unique
Personal Style!

# CONTENTS

# STYLE & YOU:
## Every Woman's Guide to Total Style

Times change. Fashions change. **You** change. The only constant thing in this dynamic world is something you create yourself: a vivid awareness of your own personal style.

What is style? It's as hard to define as "charm," "power," or "happiness" — yet you invariably know when you have achieved it. The dictionary says style is "a manner of expression characteristic of an individual." The ancient Romans had a saying, "Style reveals the inner person," and the style-conscious French amended this to "The style is the woman herself."

Style is not fashion. Fashion is a manufactured product. Style is what you do, how you live. Fashion is constantly changing. Style is unchanging, constant, an attitude of confidence and self-awareness. Style is being yourself, **on purpose.** It emanates from your central core. It is your essence.

What about **taste**? Taste is aesthetic judgment, the ability to look at the confusion of the world and select the objects, people, and experiences that are pleasing to you, that create a unified and pleasing whole. Taste is never "good" or "bad," only consistent or inconsistent. Everyone has **some** kind of taste. The taste that creates style is aware, focused, and intensely personal.

Your style is like your mind and body — partly inherited, partly self-created. Cary Grant commented that "at a certain point in my early life, I decided what sort of person I wanted to be, and over the years I've become that person." You create your own style by understanding who you are and who you want to become.

Your style is how you respond to others, your perceptiveness and ease, your caring and warmth, your ability to handle complex situations smoothly by combining basic common-sense rules with your own special awareness (this is known as "etiquette" or "savvy").

Your style is how you interpret and present the inner you to the outer world. But developing your own style can be confusing. Some doom-sayers will tell you that you either have style or you don't. They forget the most interesting part: How people with style **got** it. The person with style has consciously identified her own characteristics, organized and refined them, and ultimately shaped them into her own unique language of behavior and appearance.

**Style & You** will help you identify and develop your own personal style. There are four different style types for you to choose from in chapter one: Classic, Dramatic, Natural, Romantic. These four types are merely a guide to help you select your most dominant basic style. Once you have evaluated your basic type, you can vary your look according to the occasion. You never need feel limited or locked into just one style as it is important to create your own unique signature. In the next eleven chapters you will learn how to project the **real you** to the outside world by how you look, what you do and how you live, by the colors and fashions you choose, by your makeup, hairstyle, and fragrances. **Style & You** is your key to unlocking your own uniqueness. It is a guide to discovering **you!**

Clare Revelli in her
San Francisco Design Studio

# PART ONE

## YOUR STYLE PROFILE

# 1. PERSONAL/STYLE

CLASSIC   DRAMATIC   NATURAL   ROMANTIC

CLASSIC

DRAMATIC

NATURAL

ROMANTIC

# ASK YOURSELF:

Who am I?

What am I most comfortable doing, wearing, being?

How do I want others to perceive me?

Understanding your own personal style means understanding yourself. True style begins with personality. Does the person that others see reflect the **real you**? Or is she unfinished, haphazard, a hodgepodge of conflicting elements? Whether it be expressed by your wardrobe, the car you drive or the table setting you prefer, personal style pulls together the internal and external of your life into a harmonizing whole. It rarely just happens. Personal style must be intentionally developed and maintained.

Finding the real you doesn't mean focusing on your faults. It means throwing the spotlight on your uniqueness, identifying your strengths, then organizing and refining them into your own singular manners of behavior. The process is not only valuable and enlightening, it's fun!

True style is never "right" or "wrong." Eleanor Roosevelt wore comfortable clothes and served hotdogs to the king and queen of England. Jacqueline Kennedy dressed in Paris fashions and served gourmet cuisine to the humblest White House visitor. Both women had a unique personal style that was absolutely right for them.

There are four basic and universal personality types, no matter what is currently in fashion. Each type has variations. Note the adjectives that may apply to you on the next four pages.

# CLASSIC

Classic is:
ELEGANT
TRADITIONAL
TAILORED
CONSERVATIVE
SOPHISTICATED
FORMAL

The typical CLASSIC personality might dress in the above suit style. However, many variations exist — as listed in the above illustration. Remember: If you are a CLASSIC you may choose to vary your look with one or more of the other three styles, depending upon your personal tastes.

Dramatic is:
GLAMOROUS
EXOTIC
CREATIVE
THEATRICAL
ARTISTIC
SEXY

The typical DRAMATIC personality might dress in the above suit style. However, many variations exist — as listed in the above illustration. Reminder: If you are a DRAMATIC you may choose to vary your look with one or more of the other three styles, depending upon your personal tastes.

# NATURAL

Natural is:
CASUAL
SPORTY
INFORMAL
COUNTRY
OUTDOORSY
BASIC

The typical NATURAL personality might dress in the above suit style. However, many variations exist — as listed in the above illustration. Reminder: If you are a NATURAL you may choose to vary your look with one or more of the other three styles, depending upon your personal tastes.

Romantic is:
FEMININE
INGENUE
SOFT
VICTORIAN
DELICATE
POETIC

The typical ROMANTIC personality might dress in the above suit style. However, many variations exist — as listed in the above illustration. Reminder: If you are a ROMANTIC you may choose to vary your look with one or more of the other three styles, depending upon your personal tastes.

## EACH OF US IS A COMBINATION OF THESE FOUR STYLES.

Once you identify your **dominant** look, you can create your own individual trademark. Accessories can instantly alter your primary image. A tailored suit becomes romantic with the addition of a cameo, a chiffon scarf, or a ruffled blouse. A natural wardrobe turns dramatic when a stunning piece of jewelry or an exotic belt is added. The trick is to approach each aspect of your life with a guiding vision of your overall style.

IS YOUR PERSONALITY SHOWING?

After studying the four illustrations, review the typical personality descriptions which follow here. You may recognize one that is similar to your own personality.

The Classic Woman is a direct descendant of ancient beauties. Hers is a world of timelessness, serenity, and grace. Her refinement and savoir faire are reflected in her fabulous home, in her ready-for-anything wardrobe, in the elegant table she sets for her many guests.

The Dramatic Woman knows how to turn heads, make an entrance. She lingers in the mind long after she has departed, like a fragment of music, a haunting perfume. Her excitement and vivacity are reflected in everything around her — her decor, her parties, her conversation.

The Natural Woman reminds you of sunshine and fields of daisies, even in the moonlight. She has the gift of making everyone feel at ease. When she entertains, her guests know the conversation will be as warm and lively as the table she sets.

The Romantic Woman knows how to stir the romance and poetry in all our souls. Wherever she goes, she brings an aura of lace and bowers of flowers. In her presence voices soften, thoughts become more lyrical. An invitation to her home provides a journey to another way of life.

# HOW TO START

Think about your likes and dislikes and make a list. Thumb through clothing catalogues and magazines, noting any styles that say "you." Next take the **Style Analysis Quiz** which follows and note your answers in pencil. Refer to the answer key and illustrations of the four basic style types which will help you define your most dominant look. Remember, this is just a guide to help you decide how you will present yourself to others, how to discover the look that will eventually be reflected in all aspects of your everyday life. **(Circle only one answer for each.)**

1. The style type which best illustrates and describes my dominant look is: A. CLASSIC  B. DRAMATIC  C. NATURAL  D. ROMANTIC

2. The following statement best describes my overall fashion tastes:
   A. Tailored, understated elegance
   B. Trendsetting, different, creative
   C. Simple, comfortable, easy
   D. Soft, sensuous, feminine

3. The choice that best describes my accessories style is:
   A. Status accessories: reptile belts, skilk scarfs, etc.
   B. One-of-a-kind, bold and unusual accessories
   C. Simple items that mix and match; basic shoes and bags
   D. Ribbons, bows, lace trims and collars, ruffles

4. The choice that best describes my preference in jewelry is:
   A. Elegant and rich, yet simple
   B. Splashy, bold, sometimes ethnic
   C. All-purpose, handmade, practical
   D. Pearls, cameos, lockets or antique pieces

5. If I chose to wear a hair accessory it would be:
   A. A hat
   B. A sleek, large scale comb
   C. A tortoise headband
   D. A ribbon, bow or flower

6. The choice that best describes my preference in fabric is:
   A. Pin stripes, herringbones, tweeds
   B. Large bold prints, geometrics
   C. Checks, stripes, plaids, paisleys
   D. Tiny floral prints, gingham, dotted swiss

7. The choice that best describes my preference in shoe styles is:
   A. Spectator or plain pumps
   B. Exotic, trendy, colorful
   C. Penny loafers, topsiders
   D. Dainty straps, decorative trims

8. The choice that best describes my preference in flowers for my table setting is:
   A. Roses, carnations, orchids
   B. Antheriums, ginger, Bird of Paradise
   C. Daisies, daffodils, tulips
   D. Baby rosebuds, violets, gardenias

Once you have determined which style group best describes you, go on to Part II of this book for your best wardrobe and accessory selections.

If you are still unsure of your personal style type refer to the Style Analysis Questionnaire on page 90.

Help is nearby!

Answer Key: If you answered mostly "a", you are a "Classic"; mostly "b", "Dramatic"; mostly "c", "Natural"; mostly "d", "Romantic".

# 2. LIFE/STYLE

Your personal style is **who** you are. Your lifestyle is **what** you do. Both are part of your total image.

How and where do you currently spend your time? What is your **lifework**? Which of the following categories apply to you?

## STUDENT

Your clothes and hairstyle are fresh and fun, but with a heavy emphasis on practicality. You have more room in your life now for experimentation, fads, and fancies to relieve the grind of your studies, but they must be economical and easy to maintain.

## WORKING SINGLE

Your wardrobe and home are now a major investment. Your clothes must represent you in the business world and your home is the retreat where you establish the social relationships of your adult life. You are cautious and knowledgeable in your choices, knowing you will live with them for years to come.

## HOMEMAKER/MOTHER

Most of your energy goes into your home and family, and they glow with your attention. Unfortunately your wardrobe may begin to resemble rummage sale rejects just when you should most reflect your pride in your surroundings. You need special insights to maintain your inimitable style on a reduced income, with little time, a bouncy toddler in one hand, a paintbrush in the other, and diaper pins festooned on your shirt.

## WORKING MOTHER

Your challenge is to maintain two wardrobes, one for work and the other for work — at home. You realize that office clothes must be stripped off the minute you come through the door and replaced with comfortable, attractive, and practical outfits that work equally well for candlelit dinners, PTA meetings, cuddling the kids, and walking the dog.

## WORK IN AN OFFICE

The "Dress for Success" code is loosening its iron grip, but you are still under strong pressure to conform to what everyone else is wearing. Whether your particular office culture demands dark suits, torn blue jeans, or the cutting edge of flamboyant Paris fashion, you find ways to express your own style. You may even be able to influence and change the office styles with your example.

## WORK IN A SERVICE INDUSTRY

Nearly half of all working Americans now work in service industries and professions. If your occupation requires a uniform, you know that almost any uniform short of a Playboy bunny suit can be made to take on your personality. If you are a teacher, salesperson, bank teller, beautician, or even politician, you know you need attractive but non-threatening outfits, hairstyle, and makeup to be appealing and accessible to your public. Your choices are no less meticulous than those of the office worker.

## WORK AT HOME

More and more people are working at home, often juggling family and career under one small roof. You plan your home-office carefully, and your clothes must be ready to go from making an important presentation to a prestigious client to carpooling the soccer team. You are a quick change artist with lots of double-duty clothes and a hairstyle that goes from sophisticated to casual with just a few strokes.

## DO VOLUNTEER WORK

Helping your community is important to you. You keep a section of your closet for dresses suitable for fundraisers and attractive workclothes for sessions of helping out at the local nursing home or nursery school. Your makeup is fresh and natural by day, but quickly adapts for glamorous evenings.

## YOUR LIFEWORK

Today over 65 percent of all American women work outside the home and more are entering the labor force daily. This lifestyle transition has created major wardrobe requirements for many women. The woman who flies about the country on business may come home to an eager toddler with sticky hands. The student on a limited budget works part time in an office where traditional business attire is expected.

# LIFESTYLE

Both women may enjoy backpacking, exercise classes, gardening, or other activities that require special clothes.

Obviously your lifework, what you do and how you do it, affects what you wear and how you present yourself to others. It is directly connected to the dominant style type you selected in Chapter 1: Classic, Dramatic, Natural or Romantic. What kind of work do you do? What do you do with your free time? What types of dress-up occasions do you have in your life? What percentage of your time do you spend on work, on leisure activities, dressed up? After you answer these questions, it's time to think about how your wardrobe budget should be divided.

## YOUR LIFEWORK LIFESTYLE QUIZ

1. My lifework is _____

   (Circle one of the selections below or write one in.)

   1. Student                5. Work in office
   2. Working Single         6. Work at home
   3. Homemaker/mother       7. Work as a volunteer
   4. Working mother         8. Other _____

2. My spare time is spent _____

   1. Relaxing               8. Arts/crafts
   2. Watching television    9. Sewing
   3. Reading               10. Writing
   4. Entertaining          11. Visiting family/
   5. Cooking                   friends
   6. Sports                12. Mothering
   7. Shopping              13. Other _____

# LIFE/STYLE

3. The occasions that require me to "dress up" are:
   1. Work          4. Dining out/    6. Church
   2. Shopping          cultural events 7. Travel
   3. Luncheons 5. Entertaining      8. Other _____

4. I spend the following percentage of time in each area:
   1. Work          _____ %
   2. Casual        _____ %
   3. Dress-up      _____ %

5. My closet has the following percentage of wardrobe items:
   1. Work          _____ %
   2. Casual        _____ %
   3. Dress-up      _____ %

6. My future and new clothing investments should include the following: (Items needed in order of priority)
   1. Work          _____

   2. Casual        _____

   3. Dress-up      _____

Your personal style and your lifestyle form the basis for your **TOTAL STYLE.** This is your foundation. Now you are going to add the building blocks — color, clothing, accessories, makeup, hair, and fragrances — to form the finished you.

# 3. BODY/STYLE

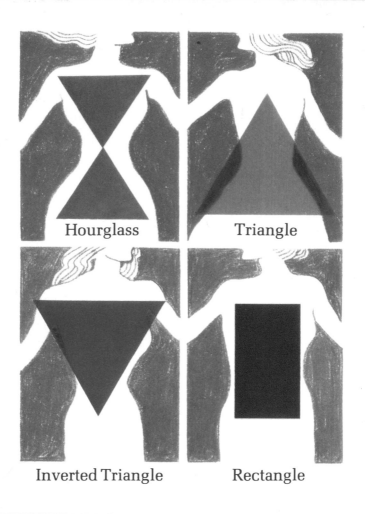

Hourglass

Triangle

Inverted Triangle

Rectangle

Four is your magic number when it comes to creating your own personal style: four fashion looks to choose from, four color groups, four body types. Your body style will strongly influence how you should select the clothes that make your statement. Three characteristics comprise one's body style: size, shape and proportion. **Size** is your height and width, **Shape** is your silhouette and **Proportion** is the length of your body sections.

To begin the process, look at these four basic figure styles and decide which describes you best. (If you're unsure, consult the nearest full-length mirror . . . or a trusted friend. Be objective.)

### HOURGLASS:

Hips and shoulders are the same width. The ideal figure for many centuries, but the full-bosomed, full-hipped woman does not always find current fashions that are kind to her curves and narrow waist.

**Objective:** To de-emphasize the extreme curves of the figure and enhance the softness of your silhouette.

### TRIANGLE:

Shoulders are narrower than hips. The most common figure type, and the least appreciated by fashion designers.

**Objective:** To de-emphasize weight below the waist and create a better balance for upper and lower body portions.

### INVERTED TRIANGLE:

Shoulders are wider than hips. MGM costume designer Adrian and Joan Crawford made this look mandatory for everyone in the 1940s.

**Objective:** To de-emphasize the upper body (above waist) and create length between the torso and legs.

### RECTANGLE:

Little or no indent at waist. Idolized in the flapper era, the rectangular figure features slim hips and a youthful bosom, a versatile framework for nearly every fashion look.

**Objective:** To de-emphasize the lack of waist and create an illusion of more indentation at the middle of torso.

# BODY/STYLE

The four basic body types described above utilize straight lines to outline the silhouette. However, the body is curved so be sure to adjust your figure shape accordingly. There are variations within each of the four body types but **everyone falls into at least one of these categories.** For instance . . . the woman who describes herself as a pear-shape would be the same as the Triangle, a heart-shape would fit into the Inverted Triangle and the very full busted and full hipped (rounded) individual would be the Rectangular type, unless her waist is quite defined whereby she would be an Hourglass. Imagining or drawing your curves on top of the four basic body types will assist you even more.

## PERFECT PROPORTIONS

A perfectly proportioned figure is eight heads tall and rare! If you took the measurement of your head from top to bottom (at your chin line) and multiplied this measurement by eight you would have your expected proportions.

Study the "perfect" proportions of the model illustrated and then compare your own figure, noting the differences. (Don't become depressed!)

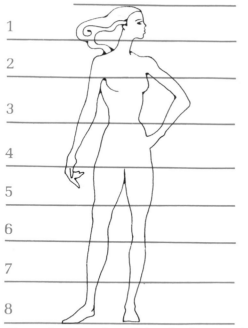

1 — Top of Head
Chinline
Base of Neck

2 — Slope of shoulder is 2" from neck base

3 — Underarm is half-way between top of head and full hip

4 — Waist is half-way between underarm and full hip

5 — Full hip or top of thighs divides body in half

6 — Hips are one inch narrower than shoulders

7 — Knee is half-way between hip and feet

8 — Soles of feet

If your shoulders slope ½" in either direction of the perfect proportion shown, you could be sloping or square.

A waist that is 1" above or below the perfect proportion will make you either short or long waisted.

If your leg length is more than 1" longer or shorter than one-half your full body length, you are either short or long legged.

26

## HOW TO MEASURE YOURSELF

Precise measurements are very important to determining your body type. Use a plastic (rather than paper) tape measure and take all measurements in your slip instead of outer clothing. Refer to profile example below.

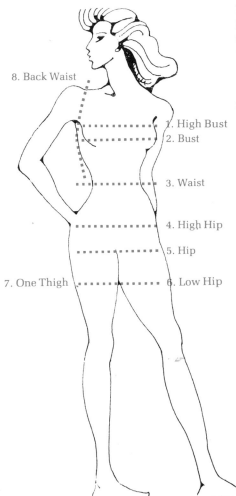

8. Back Waist

1. High Bust
2. Bust

3. Waist

4. High Hip

5. Hip

7. One Thigh

6. Low Hip

1.
**High Bust:** Measure under the arms, above the breasts and across the chest. (This number is your correct bra size. If number is odd, take the even number below it. . . i.e. 36-37 means you wear a size 36.)
2.
**Bust:** Measure across the back and over the fullest part of the bust. (When you subtract this number from your high bust measurement you will know the correct cup size to wear. *see below.

3.
**Waist:** Bend over sideways to establish your waistline. Measure the narrowest part of the torso.
4.
**High Hip:** Measure 3" down from the waist.
5.
**Hip:** Measure 7" down from the waist.
6.
**Low Hip:** With both legs together, measure around the widest part of both thighs.
7..
**Thigh:** Measure around the fullest part of one thigh.
8.
**Back Waist:** Measure from nape of neck down to waist.

*The difference between high and low bust measurements tells you the correct bra size to wear: 1-2" = A, 2-3" = B, 3-4" = C, 4-5" = D, and so on.

Now record your measurements in the figure analysis section. Continue to complete the figure analysis worksheet including your body size, shape and profile. Compare your proportions with the model's perfect shape and you should be able to determine which of the four basic body types most resembles your figure. You can pencil your shape and body type onto the model illustration to help you better visualize your silhouette.

If you are still undecided, refer to the Style Analysis Questionnaire on page 90 at the end of this book.

# FIGURE ANALYSIS WORKSHEET

## BODY SIZE
(Refer to Height/Weight chart.)

**Height:**
☐ Short (4'10" - 5'3")
☐ Average (5'4" - 5'6")
☐ Tall (5'7" and above)

**Weight:**
☐ Thin
☐ Average
☐ Heavy

## CLOTHING SIZE:
(Refer to Standard Size charts.)

_____ Junior      _____ Women's

_____ Missy       _____ Half Size

_____ Petite

## BODY SHAPE
(Refer to illustration.)

☐ Hourglass (shoulder and hip widths are balanced)
☐ Triangle (shoulders are narrow in comparison to hips)
☐ Inverted Triangle (shoulders are wide in comparison to hips)
☐ Rectangle (straight up and down with an undefined waist)

## BODY MEASUREMENTS

(Refer to model illustration on page 26.)

**Head:** ☐ Small ☐ Average ☐ Large

**Neck:** ☐ Short ☐ Average ☐ Long

**Shoulders:** ☐ Broad ☐ Average ☐ Narrow
☐ Sloped ☐ Square

**Back:** ☐ Narrow ☐ Average ☐ Wide
☐ Straight ☐ Curved

**Bust:** ☐ Small ☐ Average ☐ Large

**Arms:** ☐ Thin ☐ Average ☐ Large

**Midriff:** ☐ Flat ☐ Average ☐ Prominent

**Waist:** ☐ Small ☐ Average ☐ Large
☐ Shortwaisted ☐ Longwaisted

**Tummy:** ☐ Flat ☐ Average ☐ Full

**Hips:** ☐ Flat ☐ Average ☐ Full

**Derriere:** ☐ Flat ☐ Average ☐ Full

**Thighs:** ☐ Small ☐ Average ☐ Full

**Legs:** ☐ Short ☐ Average ☐ Long
☐ Thin ☐ Thick

## BODY PROPORTIONS

(Refer to instructions on page 27.)

_____ High Bust          _____ Hip

_____ Bust               _____ Low Hip

_____ Waist              _____ Thigh

_____ High Hip           _____ Back Waist

# STANDARD CLOTHING SIZE CHARTS
(Note: all sizes vary up to 2")

## JUNIOR

**Description:**
- 5'2" to 5'7" in height
- Short or average-waisted, with waist proportionally fuller than Missy
- Bust is smaller and higher than Missy
- Generally for a younger body, but can be any age
- Sizes 3-15

### JUNIOR SIZE CHART

| Size | 3 | 5 | 7 | 9 | 11 | 13 | 15 |
|---|---|---|---|---|---|---|---|
| Bust | 32 | 33 | 34 | 35.5 | 37 | 38 | 40 |
| Waist | 24 | 25 | 26 | 27.5 | 29 | 30 | 31 |
| Hip | 34 | 35 | 36 | 37.5 | 39 | 40 | 41 |

## MISSY

**Description:**
- 5'4" to 5'7" in height
- Average or long-waisted
- Womanly proportions
- Sizes 4-20

### MISSY SIZE CHART

| Size | 4 | 6 | 8 | 10 | 12 | 14 | 16 | 18 | 20 |
|---|---|---|---|---|---|---|---|---|---|
| Bust | 33 | 34 | 35 | 36 | 38 | 39 | 40 | 42 | 44 |
| Waist | 23 | 24 | 25 | 26 | 28 | 29 | 30 | 32 | 34 |
| Hips | 33 | 34 | 35 | 36 | 38 | 40 | 42 | 43 | 45 |

## PETITE

**Description:**
- 5'4" and under in height
- Medium or small shoulder
- Average or short waisted
- Delicate body, all ages
- Sizes 2P to 16P

### PETITE SIZE CHART

| Size | 2P | 4P | 6P | 8P | 10P | 12P | 14P | 16P |
|---|---|---|---|---|---|---|---|---|
| Bust | 32 | 33 | 34 | 35 | 36 | 38 | 39 | 41 |
| Waist | 22 | 23 | 24 | 25 | 26 | 28 | 29 | 31 |
| Hips | 33 | 34 | 35 | 36 | 37 | 38 | 40 | 41.5 |

# WOMEN'S

**Description:**
- Medium or wide shoulders
- Waist proportionally larger than Missy
- Hips somewhat fuller than bust
- Sizes 14W to 26W

### WOMEN'S SIZE CHART

| Size | 14W | 16W | 18W | 20W | 22W | 24W | 26W |
|------|-----|-----|-----|-----|-----|-----|-----|
| Bust | 39 | 41 | 43 | 45 | 47 | 49 | 51 |
| Waist | 30 | 32 | 34 | 36 | 38 | 40 | 42 |
| Hips | 40 | 42 | 44 | 46 | 48 | 50 | 52 |

# HALF SIZES

**Description:**
- 5'1'' to 5'6''
- Full bust
- Short waist
- Full tummy
- Narrow or average shoulder
- Sizes 12WP to 26WP

### PETITE SIZE CHART

| Size | 12WP | 14WP | 16WP | 18WP | 20WP | 22WP | 24WP | 26WP |
|------|------|------|------|------|------|------|------|------|
| Bust | 37 | 39 | 41 | 43 | 45 | 47 | 49 | 51 |
| Waist | 29 | 31 | 33 | 35 | 37 | 39 | 41 | 43 |
| Hips | 38 | 40 | 42 | 44 | 46 | 48 | 50 | 52 |

# STANDARD HEIGHT & WEIGHT CHART

| HEIGHT | SMALL FRAME | MEDIUM FRAME | LARGE FRAME |
|--------|-------------|--------------|-------------|
| 4'10'' | 102−111 | 109−121 | 118−131 |
| 4'11'' | 103−113 | 111−123 | 120−134 |
| 5'0'' | 104−115 | 113−126 | 122−137 |
| 5'1'' | 106−118 | 115−129 | 125−140 |
| 5'2'' | 108−121 | 118−132 | 128−143 |
| 5'3'' | 111−124 | 121−135 | 131−147 |
| 5'4'' | 114−127 | 124−138 | 134−151 |
| 5'5'' | 117−130 | 127−141 | 137−155 |
| 5'6'' | 120−133 | 130−144 | 140−159 |
| 5'7'' | 123−136 | 133−147 | 143−163 |
| 5'8'' | 126−139 | 136−150 | 146−167 |
| 5'9'' | 129−142 | 139−153 | 149−170 |
| 5'10'' | 132−145 | 142−156 | 152−173 |

# BODY/STYLE

**Best Body Bets**    HOURGLASS

- Capitalize on your evenly balanced top and bottom (jumpsuits, shirtwaist dresses, etc.).
- Show off your waist and midriff (belts, cumberbunds, etc.).
- Choose simple,soft lines that follow your curves without being too obvious (princess-style).

**Best Body Bets**    TRIANGLE

- Create an illusion of top and bottom balance (a light colored fuller-style blouse teamed with a dark mid-calf skirt, etc.).
- Emphasize your waist and midriff area (V-yoke fitted waists, belts, set-in waistbands, etc.).
- Broaden your upper torso, especially the shoulder area (full sleeves, shoulder pads, etc.).

**Best Body Bets**  INVERTED TRIANGLE

- Create the illusion of a fuller bottom torso for better balance with the upper portions (drop waist blousons, pleated or slightly gathered skirts)
- Elongate the upper torso and create the illusion of height (long scarfs, beads, banding on jackets, etc.).
- Emphasize your waist while balancing upper and lower torso to create a more hourglass effect (two-piece overblouse dress).

**Best Body Bets**    RECTANGLE

- Emphasize your hips and legs whenever possible (long cardigans, banding on jackets/sweaters).
- Elongate your figure with vertical lines (V-necks, long beads or coat dresses, etc.).
- Create the illusion of a more defined waist (elasticized waists, belts, etc.)

This is just an overview. Specific fashions for these body types are featured in Chapter 6 on Clothes.

And remember, Style is not a size. . .

# 4. FACE/STYLE

Fashion periodically favors each of the six basic face types: ROUND, SQUARE, TRIANGULAR, INVERTED TRIANGLE, RECTANGULAR and OVAL. Only the oval never seems to out of favor. If this ideal face is not your contour, take heart. By using a few tricks of the trade such as the correct makeup, a complimentary hairstyle and appropriate accessories, you can learn to enhance what nature has given you!

Your face is terrific, whatever shape you have. It is your unique signature, like no one else's. Knowing which shape you possess will further assist you in pulling together that pefect **'total style'** you are striving for.

## THE SHAPE OF YOUR FACE

Here's a frame of reference to consider in determining your face shape:

1. Look into a mirror, pulling your hair away from your face.
2. Compare the shape of your face to the illustration and note the face that most resembles yours.
3. If you are still unsure, consult a family member, friend or your hairstylist.

ROUND

Almost as wide as it is long, the round face was favored in the 1920s. The greatest width is at the cheeks and facial lines are curved.

**Goal:** To elongate the face and create angles.

SQUARE

The square (or angular) face was perfection in Roman times. It has a squared forehead about the same width as the cheekbones and jawline. The dominant feature is the squared jaw.

**Goal:** To elongate the face and soften the squareness with curves.

TRIANGULAR

The triangular (or pear-shaped) face has a jawline wider than the forehead. Cheekbones are broader than the browbone and narrower than the jawline.

**Goal:** To balance the entire face by adding width at the cheeks and forehead and minimizing the jawline.

INVERTED
TRIANGLE

Also referred to as the heart-shaped face, this contour reigned throughout the elegant 18th century. The wide forehead and high cheekbones taper to a narrow chin. (Diamond-shaped faces may also refer to combined notes of two triangular shapes.)

**Goal:** To balance the extremes of the upper and lower face portions and soften the prominent V-shape in the chinline.

RECTANGULAR

The face of Venus de Milo and Aphrodite, it has a high clear forehead, straight cheekbones and a strong, classical jawline. Also referred to as the long or narrow face, the width is greater than the length.

**Goal:** To balance, shorten, and soften the angular lines.

36

OVAL

Considered the ideal face. The forehead is wider than the chin, cheekbones are dominant, and the face tapers gracefully from cheekbones to a narrower, oval chin.
**Goal:** To maintain the natural balance and harmony of the face.

## FACING UP

Understanding your facial structure is a base from which to take off. Face shape determines three important points which you will be reading in three separate chapters of Part II, "Added Attractions":

1. The proper placement of makeup for your contour
2. The best hairstyles for your face shape
3. The most enhancing accessories (incuding eyewear) to select

# 5. COLOR/STYLE

**Primary Colors:** Red, Yellow and Blue

**Secondary Colors:** Orange, Green and Violet

**Tertiary Colors:** A mixture containing equal parts of a primary color and its neighboring secondary color

**Hue:** A pure bright color as seen in the primary and secondary colors.

**Value:** The lightness or darkness of a color determined by tinting (adding white) or shading (adding black).

**Intensity:** The strength or vividness of a hue; the brightness or dullness of a color.

Color is magic. Color is power. It's your most important ally and tool in creating your own style. More than anything else about you, it has an instant impact on others. Color surrounds you constantly, affecting your mood and energy level. With over 45 million colors to choose from, it's no wonder that even so-called experts become confused.

Simply put, colors come in two kinds: cool and warm. You can wear **any** color — it's the coolness or warmness and the darkness or lightness (shade or tint) of the color that makes the difference. Even some professional colorists do not understand this. They try to impose arbitrary rules about who can wear what, restricting and frustrating their clients. An experienced Color Consultant who has a thorough grasp of cool/warm and shade/tint knows that every client has millions of choices regardless of which 'seasonal category' one falls under. Never let anyone (including yourself!) tell you that your color selections are limited. The information that follows will easily convince you as to why your choices are limitless.

## COOL AND WARM

The cool/warm concept is the universal basis for all color systems and theories. A touch of blue ( or green or violet) in a color cools it. A touch of yellow ( or red or orange) warms it.

## SHADE AND TINT

The term **shade** means that black has been added to the actual color, thereby making it appear darker or muted.

The term **tint** means that white has been added to the actual color, thereby making it appear lighter or paler.

# THE SEASONAL COLOR CONCEPT

This unique system divides colors into nature's four seasons. Two are cool: Winter, with its striking contrasts, and Summer, with its clear translucents. Two are warm: Spring, fresh and bright, and Autumn, strong and muted.

Understanding Seasonal Color has advantages beyond expressing your image and personality. You'll quickly discover that you're saving time and money in many ways: No more clothes bought on impulse that never look quite right or go with anything else; no more drawers full of unused makeup; and no more costly decorating mistakes. And best of all, everything will mix and match perfectly as all of your color choices will be either cool or warm!

## What is Your Seasonal Type?

Your seasonal color type is determined by three factors: your skin tone, hair color, and eye color. Study them in front of a mirror and in natural daylight. Just as every color is classified as either cool or warm, so are your inherent characteristics—your skin, hair and eyes.

1. **Skin tone:** Your skin color is most important. Hair and eyes are secondary. Your skin color comes from a combination of three pigments: melanin (brown), carotene (yellow), and hemoglobin (red). A suntan may deepen your skin tone or age may fade it, but underneath, your coloring never changes.

   Look carefully at the inside of your wrist, putting a white sheet of paper underneath to prevent reflected color. Does your skin show a blue or blue-pink undertone? If so, you are cool and most likely either a Summer or a Winter type. Does your skin show a yellow or golden-beige undertone (not to be confused with sallow)? Then you are warm and either a Spring or an Autumn.

2. **Hair:** What color was your hair when you were a child? If your hair is its natural color today, does it have red or golden highlights (Spring/Autumn)? Or are the highlights ash or drab in tone (Summer/ Winter)? Even though your hair color changes naturally during your lifetime (darkens or turns gray or white with age), your seasonal type will always remain the same.

3. **Eyes:** Study your eyes in a mirror. What color is predominant? Are there gold, gray or brown flcks? If they are blue, are they more blue-gray (cool) or blue-green (warm)? Are your eyes chameleon—changing color when you wear different clothes? Does there appear to be a gray rim around the iris? Even though your eyes become lighter with age and they are the third and least important criteria in determining your seasonal type, you should note the above specifics.

## Fabric Draping To Confirm Your Season

If you are still uncertain of your seasonal color type, you can use a pair of gold and silver fabric drapes, about 12" square. Most fabric stores have this material or you may write to Revelli on the last page of this book. Pull your hair away from your face and remove your make-up. Standing in front of a mirror in **natural** daylight, first hold the silver under your chin. Study your face, not the fabric. Now take the gold fabric and do the same thing. Note which metallic fabric makes your face seem to come alive. If you are cool, the silver will make your skin glow, your hair shine and your eyes sparkle. If you are warm, the gold material will enhance you most. You may also try this with various shades and tints of red, blue, yellow or green. An orange-red is warm and seen in both Spring and Autumn's Personal Palette. A blue-red is cool and worn by both Summers and Winters. Note the four Personal Palettes in this section and how the above colors can vary. You may drape fabric or clothing in both cool and warm colors under your chin to further confirm your seasonal type. For further specifics on seasonal color you may wish to refer to my book titled **Color and You** (Pocket Books/Simon & Schuster) or the makeup and hair sections of this book.

## More Seasonal Color Notes. . .

- There are four compromise colors which all seasons can wear well: soft white, coral, light aqua or deep periwinkle blue.

- All four seasonal palettes contain neutral, or base, colors. These are found in the top row of each Personal Palette chart.

- The two cool seasons of Summer and Winter may find that some of their colors will overlap and they may want to exchange with one another occasionally. Summer's cool-based palette is generally softer and lighter than Winter's which is more vivid and deeper in comparison. The same is true for the two warm-based seasons of Spring and Autumn. They may borrow from one another from time to time but Spring's palette is clearer and brighter than Autumn's darker and more muted tones.

- Your inherited skin tone may fade with age or deepen with a suntan but your seasonal type remains the same throughout your life.

- Family members are often of the same season but may also be different. It depends upon whether the parents are of the same seasonal category and which genes the offspring inherit.

- Sallowness is a polite word for "yellow," a skin tone prevalent amongst winters and summers and occurring after age 25 or so. It must not be confused with spring's or autumn's yellow undertone which comes from their pigment of carotene.

- Although cool and warm colors can be mixed, generally this mix is not as pleasing to the eye or harmonious as colors of the same classification. This is why seasonal color for your wardrobe and environs is so wonderful . . . all of your colors coordinate and paint a harmonious picture.

- No one can be more than one season or 'a woman of all seasons' as your skin, hair and eyes are either cool or warm and your specific seasonal type is derived from this alone.

- Your **favorite** colors are not necessarily your **best** colors. . .

## Color Guidelines for the Four Personal Style types:

If you are CLASSIC, choose conservative, non-contrasting colors. The neutrals (top row) in your palette as well as shaded and muted colors befit your classic style best.

If you are DRAMATIC, you probably already prefer colors which are bold, bright and contrasted. The pure hues in your palette suit your personal style perfectly.

If you are NATURAL, you are most likely drawn to earth tones, neutrals or any one of nature's true colors. Your palette provides numerous choices for your natural tastes.

If you are ROMANTIC, consider the tints, pastels and lighter colors in your palette to coordinate best with your style lines. Whites are always appropriate for the romantic type.

Remember, no matter what your personal style is, it will be compatible with your seasonal type because there are innumerable colors to choose from.

# SELECTIONS TO CHOOSE FROM

Once you know your Personal Style type and understand the Seasonal Color concept discussed in this chapter, you will have established two major building blocks in your goal towards reaching '**total style**.'

Before referring to the seasonal charts, palettes and pictures on the following pages, take a moment to complete this easy Color Quiz. It will provide additional clues to further assist you in discovering your unique seasonal color type.

## COLOR QUIZ

1. Which group of colors do you prefer?
   A. Pure white, pure black, charcoal gray, true red, royal blue, burgundy, dark navy
   B. Soft white, rose brown, pearl gray, mauve, pastel blue, soft lavender
   C. Oyster white, dark brown, rust, olive, green, teal blue, gold, camel
   D. Peach, ivory turquoise, apricot, golden brown, bright clear yellow, medium blue, clear yellow green

2. What are your two **favorite** colors?
   (Be specific — i.e. light blue, aqua blue, blue-green, etc.)
   1. _____  2. _____

3. Name the two colors you most frequently receive compliments on (not **your** favorite colors).
   1. _____  2. _____

4. What intensity of colors do you prefer?
   A. Soft pastels or tints       C. Clear, bright and warm
   B. Bold, strong and primary    D. Muted, earthy, naturals

5. If you had to choose between pure white (no trace of yellow) and ivory which would you choose?
   A. pure white            B. ivory

6. When shopping for clothes or accessories is color a consideration?  A. yes  B. no

7. If the answer to #6 was yes, what order of priority would you place it amongst the other items on the list here? (Price, pattern/design, color, label name)

   A. _____  C. _____

   B. _____  D. _____

8. Did your mother or father surround or influence you with their color choices?

   A. _____  B. _____

Now you are ready to proceed with the next four pages and study the different seasonal types. Once you have determined which group you belong to, check Part II of this book for your best colors in makeup, hair accessories and home decor — all by your season.

If you are still unsure of your seasonal type, refer to the Color Analysis Questionnaire on page 92. Help is nearby!

Skin tone is the first and most important factor in determining your seasonal type. You can tell whether your coloring is cool or warm by observing the tone just under the skin's surface.

Study the four seasonal models here, comparing the cool women with the warm ones. Note the differences in their skin undertones.

**Clockwise:** Kathy (Spring) and Alma (Autumn) are warm with golden undertones. Silwa (Summer) and Maxine (Winter) are cool with blue undertones.

45

# SPRING

The Spring person looks best in clear, warm colors with a feeling of brightness, freshness and clarity.

Aproximately 18% of the American population are spring types. Typical heritages might include Scottish, the light Irish or more often, a mixture of several backgrounds.

Your neutrals are the first five colors in the top row.

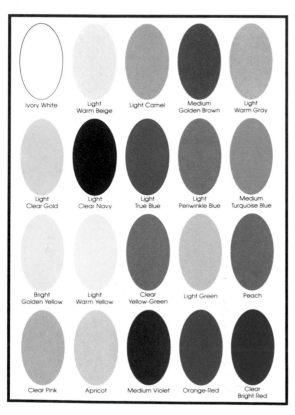

| | | | | |
|---|---|---|---|---|
| Ivory White | Light Warm Beige | Light Camel | Medium Golden Brown | Light Warm Gray |
| Light Clear Gold | Light Clear Navy | Light True Blue | Light Periwinkle Blue | Medium Turquoise Blue |
| Bright Golden Yellow | Light Warm Yellow | Clear Yellow-Green | Light Green | Peach |
| Clear Pink | Apricot | Medium Violet | Orange-Red | Clear Bright Red |

## CHARACTERISTICS:

### SKIN
Golden Beige Undertone Ivory, Peach, Peach Pink, Light or Gold Beige
Freckles: Light Golden Brown

### HAIR
Yellow or Golden Blond, Blond-Red, Strawberry Blond/ Redhead, Auburn, Golden Brown, Golden Gray

### EYES
Clear/Bright Blue, Aqua, Blue with Turquoise, Bluish Green, Clear Green, Light Brown, Golden/Topaz Brown

# SUMMER

The Summer person looks best in cool, soft, muted colors, pastels and tints of sea-and-sky tones.

There are more summer types in the United States than any other season, comprising aproximately 40% of the population. They often come from Scandinavian or German families; others have English, Australian or Dutch ancestors.

Your neutrals are the first five colors in the top row.

## CHARACTERISTICS:
### SKIN
Blue Undertone
Light Beige (tinge of pink),
Light Beige (a bit pale),
Rosy Pink (translucent)
Freckles: Med. to Dark Brown

### HAIR
Platinum, Ash and Smoky
Blond, Smoky Brown
(reddish cast), Dark Brown
(taupe cast), Blue-Gray

### EYES
Clear/Sky Blue, Gray-Blue, Pale Gray, Green, Hazel (blue/brown or green/brown), Soft Brown

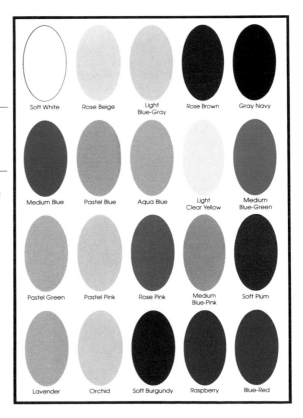

| Soft White | Rose Beige | Light Blue-Gray | Rose Brown | Gray Navy |
| Medium Blue | Pastel Blue | Aqua Blue | Light Clear Yellow | Medium Blue-Green |
| Pastel Green | Pastel Pink | Rose Pink | Medium Blue-Pink | Soft Plum |
| Lavender | Orchid | Soft Burgundy | Raspberry | Blue-Red |

# AUTUMN

The Autumn person should wear rich, warm earthen colors with golden undertones.

The Autumn types are the most rare of all seasons as there are only about 8% found in the United States. They come from a variety of national backgrounds but especially from families of Irish and Scottish backgrounds.

Your neutrals are the first five colors in the top row.

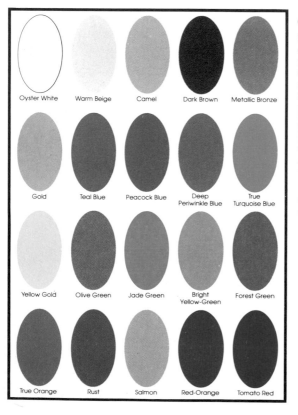

| Oyster White | Warm Beige | Camel | Dark Brown | Metallic Bronze |
| Gold | Teal Blue | Peacock Blue | Deep Periwinkle Blue | True Turquoise Blue |
| Yellow Gold | Olive Green | Jade Green | Bright Yellow-Green | Forest Green |
| True Orange | Rust | Salmon | Red-Orange | Tomato Red |

**CHARACTERISTICS:**

**SKIN**
Golden Beige Undertone
Ivory, Peach, Golden Beige, Copper Beige, Golden Black
Freckles: Gold/Blond or Light Brown

**HAIR**
Red, Reddish Brown, Golden Brown, Golden Blond, Charcoal Black, Bronze or Metallic Gray

**EYES**
Dark Brown, Golden Brown, Yellow-Brown, Hazel, Deep to Pale Green, Jade Green, Peacock Blue

# WINTER

The Winter person shines in in the vivid primary colors, cool icy tones and sharply contrasting black and white.

Winter types are quite common, comprising about 34% of the country's population. Their ethnic origins may include Asian, Black, Mediterranean, Latin American, East Indian, Middle Eastern, and even the "dark" Irish.

Your neutrals are the first six colors in the top two rows.

## CHARACTERISTICS:

### SKIN
Blue Undertone
Milk White, White (red/rose undertone), Beige, Rosy Beige, Olive (light to dark), Black
Freckles: Dark Brown

### HAIR
Black (blue cast), Brown (med. to dark), White Blond, Salt and Pepper, Silver-Gray, White (snow)

### EYES
Black, Dark Brown, Brown (reddish), Hazel, Green (white flecks), Gray, Medium Blue, Dark Blue

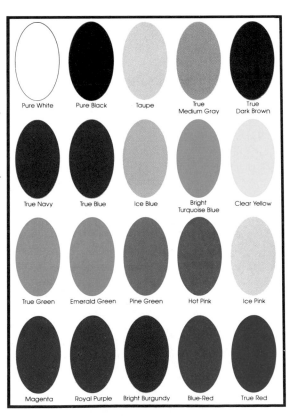

| Pure White | Pure Black | Taupe | True Medium Gray | True Dark Brown |
| True Navy | True Blue | Ice Blue | Bright Turquoise Blue | Clear Yellow |
| True Green | Emerald Green | Pine Green | Hot Pink | Ice Pink |
| Magenta | Royal Purple | Bright Burgundy | Blue-Red | True Red |

# STYLE PROFILE

## SCORECARD

Please review each of the five sections below and circle or write one in that best describes YOU based on what you have learned thus far.

I.  PERSONAL/STYLE
   A.  CLASSIC (also known as: Elegant, Traditional, Tailored, Conservative, Sophisticated, Formal)
   B.  DRAMATIC (also known as: Glamorous, Exotic, Creative, Theatrical, Artistic, Sexy)
   C.  NATURAL (also known as: Casual, Sporty, Informal, Country, Outdoorsy, Basic)
   D.  ROMANTIC (also known as Feminine, Ingenue, Soft, Victorian, Delicate, Poetic)
   My basic style is _____

II.  LIFE/STYLE
   A.  Student            E.  Work in an Office
   B.  Working Single     F.  Work in a Service Industry
   C.  Homemaker/         G.  Work at Home
       Mother            H.  Work as a Volunteer
   D.  Working Mother     I.  Other: _____
   My basic lifework is _____

III.  BODY/STYLE
   A.  HOURGLASS       C.  INVERTED TRIANGLE
   B.  TRIANGLE        D.  RECTANGLE
   My basic body type is _____

IV.  FACE/STYLE
   A.  ROUND
   B.  SQUARE (or angular)
   C.  TRIANGULAR (or pear-shaped)
   D.  INVERTED TRIANGLE (or heart, diamond)
   E.  RECTANGULAR (or long, narrow)
   F.  OVAL
   My basic face shape is _____

V.  COLOR/STYLE
   A.  SPRING (warm)   C.  AUTUMN (warm)
   B.  SUMMER (cool)   D.  WINTER (cool)
   My seasonal type is _____

*You can receive further assistance in determining your basic style/type by completing the analysis questionnaires on pages 90-93 in the back of this book.

# PART TWO

## ADDED ATTRACTIONS

# 6. CLOTHES

# CLOTHES

You **can** look terrific. No matter what your size, shape, budget, or lifestyle, there are dozens of exciting outfits that are absolutely right for you and your own unique personal style.

You've determined your dominant personal style, lifestyle, body type, face shape, and seasonal color group. Now you are ready to select the clothes that will become your signature.

Your clothes should reflect and be in harmony with:

- your personality
- your lifework
- where and how you live
- your body type
- your face shape
- your color group

Anything that you choose to wear is an extension of both your body and your psyche. Whether it's a ballgown, bathrobe, or bathing suit, you are broadcasting exactly how you feel about yourself and about where you are, what you're doing, and who you're doing it with.

Dressing with **style** is very different from dressing in **fashion**. Fashions are followed by people who do not know who they are and who depend on others to create their identity for them. Style is making a personal statement about yourself. Fashion is timely. Style is timeless. When you develop your own personal style, you tell the world "I am comfortable, confident, I know who I am." Once you know your **basic** self, you can enhance, accessorize, and create your own individual look.

With so much to choose from, it's easy to get confused. Start by making a list of what you like and dislike in clothes (i.e., dress pants, jackets, etc.) Then thumb through magazines and catalogues, noting the fashions that say "you." Consider the three design basics that follow.

CLOTHES

## THREE DESIGN BASICS

Everything you wear possesses three qualities: line, texture, and color.

**Line** is the two-dimensional space between two points. The most common lines are:

Vertical ● Horizontal ● Diagonal ● Curved ● Motion

Most designers start with line — a sketch or line drawing — to create new fashions. Then they consider the texture.

**Texture** is the character of the fabric a garment is made with. The kind of fibers (wool, silk, cotton, etc.) and the pattern in which the fibers are woven (twill, crepe, broadcloth, etc.) determine how the fabric feels and falls.
● **feel** — smooth, rough, soft, hard
● **light-reflecting** — matte, shiny, high-sheen, sparkly
● **weight** — sheer, light, medium, heavy, bulky
● **stiffness** — fluid, soft, firm, crisp

The designer chooses the fabric that will best emphasize the lines of the garment — swirling, floating, draping, flaring. The final step is adding the color to the sketch.

**Color** stimulates the eye and the brain. In clothing design, three variations of color are considered:

1. light or bright :
   to emphasize features

2. dark or muted :
   to minimize features

3. contrasting :
   to divert the eye and change proportions.

Remember to refer to your seasonal color group whenever considering this design basic. All seasonal palettes offer the three variations discussed above. Color can be used to balance or reproportion specific features or the whole figure.

## USING LINE

All garments have both outside and inside lines. The outside lines are the silhouette or shape that the garment gives your body, what you look like from a distance. The inside lines are formed by strong design elements within the silhouette. If you're unclear about this, draw a line around the outside of a fashion photo or illustration in a magazine. This will assist you in recognizing both outside and inside lines.

Outside Lines (Silhouette)　　Inside Lines

(Seams, braid, contrasting inserts, a line of buttons, ruffles, belt collar, zipper, or fabric print)

## OUTSIDE LINES

Some silhouettes look better with your proportions than others. You should be able to easily recognize the shape. Study the following illustrations and note which of the four basic body types are depicted by the outside line of the silhouette.

Clothing examples of four basic silhouettes (outside lines)

   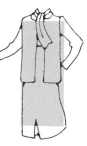

HOURGLASS    TRIANGLE    INVERTED TRIANGLE    RECTANGLE

The following chart shows your best bets for outside lines. (But every body type can wear any silhouette provided **fit** is correct.) Refer to your Figure Analysis Worksheet in Body/Style chapter.

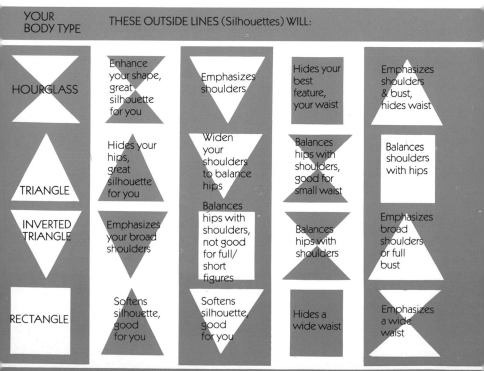

| YOUR BODY TYPE | THESE OUTSIDE LINES (Silhouettes) WILL: | | | |
|---|---|---|---|---|
| HOURGLASS | Enhance your shape, great silhouette for you | Emphasizes shoulders | Hides your best feature, your waist | Emphasizes shoulders & bust, hides waist |
| TRIANGLE | Hides your hips, great silhouette for you | Widen your shoulders to balance hips | Balances hips with shoulders, good for small waist | Balances shoulders with hips |
| INVERTED TRIANGLE | Emphasizes your broad shoulders | Balances hips with shoulders, not good for full/short figures | Balances hips with shoulders | Emphasizes broad shoulders or full bust |
| RECTANGLE | Softens silhouette, good for you | Softens silhouette, good for you | Hides a wide waist | Emphasizes a wide waist |

## INSIDE LINES

Less obvious than the outside lines, inside lines form the design details of a garment. They can be formed by seams, braid, contrasting inserts, a line of buttons, a ruffle or peplum, belt, collar, zipper, pocket opening, or by the printed or woven pattern of the fabric. Practice will teach you to identify inside lines. Remember the five lines you are looking for: vertical, horizontal, diagonal, curved, and motion.

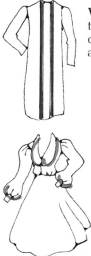

**Vertical Lines**
take the eye up and down to lengthen and narrow

**Horizontal Lines**
take the eye across to widen

**Curved Lines**
create the same effect as the vertical or horizontal lines closest to it

**Diagonal Lines**
can lengthen or shorten depending upon placement

**Motion Lines**
can slim or widen depending upon placement

## USING TEXTURE

Texture defines your mood and movements. Whatever your body type is, you can balance your shape
by using light, soft, and matte-textured fabrics that
de-emphasize figure flaws. Rough, thick, and shiny
fabrics make you look fuller. The following chart shows
your best bets for textures.

| Light Textures | Fabric Names | Effect |
| --- | --- | --- |
| Soft, drapey | Wool jersey, challis, tissue faille | Drapes over your curves, slims if a loose style |
| Soft, clingy | Silk jersey, charmeuse, de chine | Closely follows curves of body |
| Soft, floaty | Voile, organza, batiste | Stands away from the body, emphasizes movement |
| Smooth, medium firmness | Lightweight gabardine, broadcloth, silk twill | Flatters the figure |
| Matte, soft | Challis, flannel | Figure appears smaller because fabric aborbs light |

| Medium Textures | Fabric Names | Effect |
| --- | --- | --- |
| Shiny | Charmeuse, satin, taffeta | Emphasizes and enlarges the body by reflecting light |
| Rough, crisp | Linen, poplin, gabardine, pique, denim | Doesn't cling. May conceal flaws. |

| Heavy Textures | Fabric Names | Effect |
| --- | --- | --- |
| Bulky | Mohair, coatings, bulky knits, boucles, fur | Enlarges silhouette, will conceal flaws, should be used carefully by smaller figures |
| Napped | Velour, corduroy | Enlarges silhouette, may emphasize flaws, should be used carefully by larger figures |
| Coarse | Tweeds, nubbed wools | Enlarges silhouette, may conceal flaws |

## DO's and DON'Ts

Whether you are short, tall, thin or heavy, you can use line, texture, and color to create the illusion of harmonious proportions. The following DOs and DON'Ts will help you select your best looks.

If you are SHORT or PETITE, dress to elongate.

DO                                                    DON'T

## IF YOU ARE SHORT (UNDER 5'3"):

| | DOs | DON'Ts |
|---|---|---|
| **Necklines** | Deep V or oval | Very wide |
| **Sleeves** | Short or slim | Full or bulky |
| **Tops** | Slim, close-fitting | Heavy or elaborate |
| **Jackets** | Short and slim | Long or full |
| **Belts** | Narrow or none | Wide |
| **Skirts** | Slim or A-line | Too full or long |
| **Colors** | Monochromatic (all shades of same color) | Too much contrast |
| **Fabrics & Textures** | Crisp, matte textures, soft, sleek flat finishes | Bulky, large patterns, plaids, or stripes, shiny materials |

If you are TALL and THIN, dress to widen and soften.

DO          DON'T

# CLOTHES

## IF YOU ARE TALL (OVER 5'7"):

|  | DOs | DON'Ts |
| --- | --- | --- |
| **Necklines** | High, wide, soft | Deep V or very bare |
| **Sleeves** | Full, 3/4, or long | Sleeveless |
| **Tops** | Full or bloused | Flat or tight |
| **Jackets** | Loose, bulky, big collars | Too short or tight |
| **Belts** | Wide | Beltless or too narrow |
| **Skirts** | Slim or full, not too long | Long and narrow |
| **Colors** | Light, two-tones | Too heavy or dull |
| **Fabrics & Textures** | Light, soft, deep-piled bulky wools, nubby tweeds, boucles, large prints | Flat, dull-finished, hard-textured, clingy |

## IF YOU ARE EXTRA THIN:

### DOs

Congratulations! The fashion designers had you in mind when they sat down at the drawing board. However, if you want to minimize your slenderness, go for heavier-weight and highly textured fabrics (unless you are extremely short), horizontal lines, blouson bodices, fuller skirts.   Look for details, such as ruffles, gathers, tucks, yokes and pockets.

### DON'Ts

Vertical lines, no belt, dark hosiery.

## IF YOU ARE EXTRA HEAVY:

### DOs

Softer, lighter-weight fabrics in medium or dark colors, vertical lines. Create a focal point around your face and enhance with important jewelry and scarves, the right color choices, and makeup. If you have a well-defined waist, try a dramatic belt. (Choose clothes that are a little

# CLOTHES

loose — people will constantly compliment you on losing weight!)

**DON'Ts**

Stiff, super-clingy, or shiny fabrics; gaudy colors, prints, or plaids (but don't be afraid to experiment in front of the mirror — a smart bias-cut plaid may take 20 pounds off); accessories on too small a scale (like tiny chains and handbags); anything too tight or ill-fitting.

## FLATTERING YOUR FIGURE FLAWS

| If your flaw is... | These styles should flatter... |
| --- | --- |
| Short Neck | V or U-necks, open collars, scooped or square necklines, cardigan jackets, long pointed collars or lapels, camisoles |
| Long Neck | Turtlenecks, cowl or high necklines, boat necklines, Mandarin, Victorian, and high collars, ruffles at neck, one-shoulder evening dresses, hairstyles that cover the nape of the neck, scarfs, necklaces, etc. at neckline |
| Broad Shoulders | Triangle-shaped silhouettes (Tents), full skirts, V or U-scoop necklines, convertible, shawl collars, dolman, raglan, dropped shoulder, halters, strapless tops, narrow lapels |
| Narrow Shoulders | Padded or extended shoulders, set-in sleeves, drop shoulders, puffed sleeves, cap sleeves, leg-o-mutton sleeves, small collars, V, square or bateau necklines, horizontal yokes, boxy jackets, boleros |
| Sloping Shoulders | Padded shoulders, set-in and puffed sleeves, boat necks, yokes |
| Small Bust | Easy, flowing blouses, blouson tops, tucked or draped blouses, Empire waistlines, vests, bolero jackets, neckline interest; soft bow, jabot, patch pockets, ruffles, cowl neckline, longer, slightly flared A-line or straight skirts |
| Full Bust | A-line, shift, shirtwaist, loose tops, V-necks, shawl, convertible, open collars, soft shirts, cardigan and Chanel jackets |
| Short Waist | V-necks, tunics, overblouses, loose layers, longer open vests and jackets, blouson style blouse or dress, A-line, shift and princess styles, dropped waistline, slacks that ride on natural waist |
| Long Waist | A-line, shift, empire styles, full gathered skirts, skirts just below the knee, separates, short jackets, vests, sweaters, wide belts, fitted waistbands |
| Thick Waist | Chanel-type jackets, Princess, A-line, shift, chemise, tent styles, Blouson drop waists, vests, loose waistlines, tunic tops, wide or wrap belts |

# CLOTHES

| | |
|---|---|
| **Small Waist** | Overblouses, jackets with unfitted waistlines, pleated or gathered skirts, belted tunics, belts which focus attention on waist |
| **Heavy Arms** | Raglan, dolman, kimono, bishop, peasant sleeves, wide armhole cuts, long unbroken sleeve lines, no cuffs, loose fitting jackets, layers. |
| **Thin Arms** | Draped or bulky sleeves, horizontal lines in sleeves, wide sleeves, fullness above elbow, bishop, leg-o-mutton sleeves, elbow length sleeves with no cuffs |
| **Full tummy** | A-line skirts with soft inverted front pleats, trousers with soft pleats, chemises, loose-fitting waistless dresses, overblouses, tunics, long vests, box-style jackets |
| **Full hips (or thighs)** | Inverted-pleat-A-line skirt, wrap skirt, button front A-line, flared bias or gored skirts, cardigan jackets |
| **Small Hips** | Pleated, dirndl, gathered, peg-topped skirts, Flapper-style loose dresses, loose pleated slacks, harem pants, overshirts, belted overblouses, pants with side pockets and details |
| **Full Derriere** | Long vests, loose slacks, slacks and skirts in simple designs, dress style that falls from the shoulders or arms, caftans, chemises, softly pleated and dirndl skirts |
| **Flat Derriere** | Two-piece dresses, gored skirts, pants and skirts pleated or gathered at waist, culottes, harem pants, hip pockets, short vests |
| **Short Legs** | Wear waist above natural waistline, narrow or long skirts (worn with boots), shorter jackets and sweaters, higher heels, loose trousers — long, straight-leg, vertical lines |
| **Long Legs** | Long sweaters, tunics, tiered or ruffled skirts, ankle length pants, lower heeled shoes |
| **Heavy Legs** | Straight dirndl (worn over the knee), straight-leg slacks, boots, simple shoe designs, matching shoes, hose, and skirt/dress, darker shades of hose |
| **Thin Legs** | Light-colored hose, skirts at calf-length or knee length, low-heeled shoes |

# CLOTHES

## CLOTHING • YOUR STYLE...

In maintaining your unique personal style type, you may wish to refer to the style selections listed below. Use this as a guideline before going shopping and to insure that your total image is in harmony with your clothes.

### CLASSIC

**Dresses:** Soft sheaths, shirtwaists, tailored wraps, coatdresses, straight-style flat knits
**Skirts:** Soft or straight line, softly pleated, wrap or inverted pleat style, A-line
**Jackets:** Chanel-style, cardigan, blazers, smooth straight lines, double- breasted
**Pants:** Pleated or plain front, minimum detailing, straight leg
**Blouses:** Shirtmaker/tailored, stock-tie with bow, jewel neckline

### DRAMATIC

**Dresses:** Coatdresses, chemises, slinky sheaths, soft asymmetrical or bias cuts, sculpted shoulders and shoulder pads
**Skirts:** Straight, narrow, longer, bias cuts, tulip or trumpet, asymmetrical styles
**Jackets:** Unconstructed, short or long cardigan styles, single-button, hip-band, or peplum style
**Pants:** Leather, soft pleated man-tailored, harem, tapered or unconstructed, pajama or palazzo style
**Blouses:** Billowy, blouson, unconstructed, ethnic styles

### NATURAL

**Dresses:** Wrap or safari styles, T-shirt or two-piece styles
**Skirts:** Dirndl, pleated, softly tailored, culottes, simple straight styles
**Jackets:** Longer, unconstructed, easy fit and notched lapels, long cardigan, minimal padding at shoulders
**Pants:** Simple styles, drawstring, elasticized and unconstructed, all lengths
**Blouses:** Patch-pocket/safari, convertible open collared, Peter Pan collar, softly tailored shirtmaker, unconstructed

### ROMANTIC

**Dresses:** Feminine, flowing, soft and full styles. Details such as ruffles, frills, flounces
**Skirts:** Soft, full, flowing, trumpet, bias-cut or gored styles
**Jackets:** Waist-fitted, peplums, soft shoulder padding, ruffle, shirring or gathering for details and trim
**Pants:** Waist-gathered or pegged bottom, draped styles
**Blouses:** Gathered, Victorian or peasant styles, shawl, cowl, or draped collars, details such as ruffles, lace, scallops

# CLOTHES

## CLOTHING • YOUR BODY TYPE...

It is a good idea to also take into consideration your body type when making clothing decisions. As you already have noted your particular shape, consider the suggestions listed under your specific type for additional guidelines. Refer to the Style Glossary in this section for further interpretation.

### HOURGLASS

**Dresses:** Princess, drop waist, shirtwaist, chemise, coat dress, wrap
**Skirts:** Straight, trumpet, A-line, wide pleats, circle, split style
**Jackets:** Blazer, Spencer, safari, peplum, tuxedo, bolero
**Pants:** Straight or peg leg, cropped, knicker or culotte, harem, pleated trousers
**Blouses:** Collarless, notched, convertible, button down, bateau, Peter Pan, shawl collar

### TRIANGLE

**Dresses:** Surplice, A-line, float, drop-waist, A-line coat dress, set-in waist, princess, empire
**Skirts:** Box, knife or side pleat, gored, gathered, circle, Gaucho, split styles
**Jackets:** Blazer, Spencer, safari, peplum, bolero, fitted styles
**Pants:** Wide leg short, pleated trousers, palazzo, harem, culotte, hip yoke
**Blouses:** Poet, Victorian, surplice, peasant, cowl, bateau, mandarin

### INVERTED TRIANGLE

**Dresses:** Shirtwaist, drop-waist or straight lines, two-piece blouson, chemise
**Skirts:** Gathered, flared at bottom, trumpet, kick pleat
**Jackets:** Pea jacket, semi-fitted, capes, smock-styles
**Pants:** Tap pants, pull-on elastic waist, hip yoke, cropped, tailored with hip details
**Blouses:** Blouson, collarless button front, cardigan, tunic, overblouses, sailor-style

### RECTANGLE

**Dresses:** Princess, chemise, empire or drop-waist styles, two-piece overblouse, tunic dress, coat dress, A-line
**Skirts:** A-line, bias, kick or inverted pleat, wrap, split
**Jackets:** Blazer, Spencer, safari, tuxedo, blouson, shoulder padding in all styles
**Pants:** Straight leg, cropped, hip yoke, pleated trouser, peg leg
**Blouses:** Bateau, peasant, poet, notched-convertible, tunic, overblouse

# CLOTHES

## DRESSES

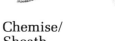

Chemise/
Sheath     Fitted
Waist     Princess/
A-Line     Tent

Shirtdress    Shirtwaist    Empire    Blouson

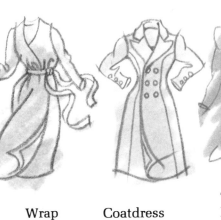

Dropped
Waist    Wrap    Coatdress    Tunic
Dress

# CLOTHES

## SKIRTS

Straight

A-Line

Dirndl

Gathered/
Flared

Wrap

Pleated

Gored

Trumpet

## PANTS

Straight leg

Pleated

Culottes

Palazzo/Pajama

Hip Yoke

Jeans

Elastic or Drawstring

Harem

# CLOTHES

## JACKETS

Bolero

Chanel/
Cardigan

Blazer

Peplum

Spencer

Safari

## VESTS

Long

Short Fitted

## BLOUSES/NECKLINES

| Jewel | Scoop | U | V |
|---|---|---|---|
| Square | Bateau/ Boat | Sweetheart | Cowl |
| Draped | Halter | Crew | Turtle |
| Peter Pan | Convertible | Shawl | Mandarin |

# 7. FABRICS

# FABRICS

Fabric is your second skin, a sensuous extension of your body. It caresses and defines your shape. You are keenly aware of how it feels as well as how it looks. Combining the right fabric with the right design that is **right** for your personality and body type is what your personal style is all about.

Start noticing the fabrics around you, how they feel and look. Are they sleek, shaggy, soft, stiff? Do they draw you to them or repel you? The feel and look of a fabric comes from many factors: the kind of fibers it is made from, the thickness and twist of the threads, the weave, the affects of dyeing, and the finishing processes at the mill.

**Fibers** come in two kinds: natural (from an animal or plant, like silk, cotton, wool, linen) or man-made (polyesters, Nylon, Orlon, Dacron, etc.) Natural fibers tend to be more comfortable because they "breathe." Artificial fibers generally wear longer, fade less, may wrinkle less and be easier to keep clean.

## NATURAL FIBERS

| | |
|---|---|
| wool (including Alpaca, camel hair, vicuna, cashmere, mohair) | linen (flax) cotton silk |

## MAN-MADE FIBERS (most commonly used)

| | |
|---|---|
| acetate | polyester |
| acrylic | rayon |
| metallic | rubber |
| modacrylic | spandex |
| nylon | vinyl |

There are eight different types of fabric construction possible, however the two most commonly used methods are known as woven and knitted. Other techniques include netting, crocheting, braiding, felting, bonding and malimo.

**Weaves** are how the threads are formed into cloth. Most commonly they are either knit or woven. Knit fabrics are made of interlocking loops. Some common variations are jerseys, tricots, ribbed knits, and double knits. Knits stretch in all directions.

Woven fabrics are produced on a loom, with the individual threads going under and over in different patterns to produce the various weaves: plain, basketweave, twill, satin, and

# FABRICS

piled fabrics like velvet and corduroy.

**Dyeing and finishing** use heat, chemicals, and pressure on the fabric, affecting its stiffness and surface.

## NATURAL FABRICS:

| FABRIC | ADVANTAGES | DISADVANTAGES |
|---|---|---|
| **Wool** Gabardines, flannel, tweed, crepe, jersey, merino | Wears well, tightly woven, smooth surface, fibers breathe and insulate, can be molded, holds shape, wrinkles hang out, provides natural warmth, has good dye affinity. | Expensive, shows sheen from press marks, press cloth is a must, dry-clean only. Limited abrasion resistance, weakens and stretches when wet, weakened by sunlight, can shrink and pill, mildews if damp. |
| **Linen** (flax) | Durable, natural luster, wears well, does not pill, absorbent, available in sheer, medium or heavy, does not lint, excellent absorbency, carries heat from body. | Wrinkles easily, loses body after several cleanings, poor affinity for dyes, may bleed, will shrink unless treated, best to dry-clean, launder if pre-shrunk, shows wear at edges and folds. |
| **Cottons:** Broadcloth, poplin, organdy, terry, corduroy, seersucker, denim, jersey, pique, oxford cloth. | Washable, inexpensive, strong, does not pill, absorbent, carries heat from body, holds color, no static electricity. | Tendency to wrinkle, shrinks badly if not treated, weakened by sunlight, can mildew. |
| **Silks:** Crepe de chine, broadcloth, chiffon, brocade, satin, jersey, organza | Drapes beautifully, has deep luster, hand washes well, available in variety of weaves, knits and weights, brilliant color dyes, wrinkle resistant, absorbent, holds body heat, resists mildew, moths. | Expensive, must hand-wash or dry-clean, may cling from static electricity, weakened by sunlight and perspiration, may yellow, fade with age. |

# FABRICS

## MAN-MADE FABRICS:

| FABRIC | ADVANTAGES | DISADVANTAGES |
|---|---|---|
| **Acrylic:**<br>Sheers, knits, fleece, furlike and pile fabrics | Soft, lightweight, wrinkle resistant, quick drying, washable, color-fast, resists mildew, moths, chemicals, sunlight, holds pleats and shape, heat sensitive, inexpensive. | May pill, can accumulate static electricity. |
| **Acetate:**<br>Satin, jersey, taffetas, tricot, brocade, lace, crepes | Holds color, resists mildew and moths, holds body heat, resists stretching and shrinking, inexpensive. | Accumulates static electricity, not very strong, weakened by light, tendency to wrinkle. |
| **Nylon:**<br>Woven and knits, jersey, many blends | Wrinkle resistant, strong, washes easily, low absorbency, can be heat-set to hold shape, resists moths and mildew, elastic qualities. | Can fade, can melt under high heat, may pill, does not breathe in hot climates, accumulates static electricity. |
| **Polyester:**<br>Broadcloth, gabardine, crepe de chine, knits | Excellent wrinkle and abrasion resistance, wash and wear, high strength, draping qualities, low absorbency — may hold in body heat, color-fast, resists mildew, resists stretching and shrinking. | Has static electricity, has seam slippage, may yellow with age, may pill and pick up lint, does not breath in hot climates. |
| **Rayon:**<br>Wovens and knits, many blends | Can resemble natural fibers, available in lightweight and heavy-weight, drapes well, comfortable, absorbent, holds body heat, inexpensive. | Not a strong fiber, weaker when wet, wrinkles, weakened with prolonged sun-light, can ravel if wet, dry clean only. |

## TEXTURES AND FABRICS FOR YOUR STYLE...

As you noted in the preceding chapter on clothes, your style type should be taken into consideration whenever making a wardrobe purchase. The same applies to your fabric and texture selections. The following will serve as another guideline for maintaining your correct look according to your personal style.

## CLASSIC
Matte finish, smooth or slight sheen: linen, raw silk, cashmere, wool gabardine or flannel, crepe, shantung, chiffon, satin, velvet, tweeds, twills.

## DRAMATIC
Shiny, glittery, tightly woven: silk jacquard, raw silk, wool jersey, lame, silk faille, leather, stiff brocades, heavy satins, patterned velveteens, velours.

## NATURAL
Flat, smooth, soft, crinkled: cotton, denim, canvas, seersucker, cable knit, corduroy, camel hair, wool flannel, tweed, silk, taffeta, velour, plain knits.

## ROMANTIC
Soft, smooth or plush: angora, tissue linen, sheer wool or crepe, cashmere, rayon, chiffon, lace, voile, challis, jersey, shantung, batiste, peau de soie, velvet, organza.

## TEXTURES FOR YOUR BODY TYPE...
All four of the body types can wear almost any fabric, it's the texture that will create the illusion you are seeking. As you learned in the previous chapter, texture in a fabric is comprised of feel, light-reflection, weight and stiffness. The chart will assist you further in selecting the right fabrics for your specific body type.

## HOURGLASS
Feel: smooth or soft; Light-reflection: matte or high sheen; Weight: light or medium; Stiffness: fluid, soft or crisp.

## TRIANGLE
Feel: smooth, soft or hard; Light-reflection: matte, shiny, high sheen; Weight: light or medium; Stiffness: firm or crisp.

## INVERTED TRIANGLE
Feel: smooth, rough or soft; Light-reflection: matte, shiny high sheen; Weight: medium; Stiffness: fluid, soft

## RECTANGLE
Feel: smooth or soft; Light-reflection: matte, shiny high sheen; Weight: light; Stiffness: fluid, soft

# 8. ACCESSORIES

Accessories are your trademark. They are like the frosting on the cake. Most of the energy has gone into the cake itself, but the frosting makes the first impression. The term accessories covers necessities like shoes, watches, eyeglasses, and handbags, and options like hats, barrettes, scarves, necklaces, earrings, brooches, rings, bracelets, combs, clips, flowers, belts, shawls, and gloves. Using the first seven chapters of this book, you have carefully built the structure of your personal wardrobe style. Now you are going to add the finishing touches to your clothes.

You have the most freedom (and therefore the most choice and potential confusion) when you select your accessories. This is one area where the four personality types blur. A basically Dramatic woman can turn Classic at a board meeting by adding an understated scarf, pin, and belt to a red jersey dress. The Natural woman shows her Romantic nature on a special evening with a flowered picture hat and cameo earrings. Don't be afraid to experiment by drawing from one of the other personality types — depending upon your mood and the occasion! This is your chance to be creative and let your signature stamp show. But don't forget to stay within your seasonal color palette. Refer to the illustrations and charts on the following pages for accessory advice in your style, season and shape.

## STYLE ACCESSORY SUGGESTIONS

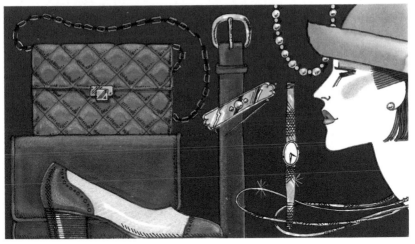

### CLASSIC
Clean, simple, elegant styles: pearls, gold or silver chains, stud or button earrings, basic watch style, bar pins, smooth grain, slim, narrow belts, Chanel-style bag, derby or fedora hat, medium-heeled pumps.

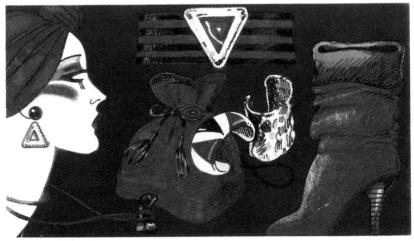

### DRAMATIC
Striking, unusual, bold styles: ethnic, asymmetrical or oversized earrings, avant-garde watch style, one-of-a-kind or wearable art brooches, bold buckled, wide, metallic, or handmade belts, lame, faux-gem, geometric shaped bags, turbans, snoods, or skull caps, high-heeled, strappy shoes or boots.

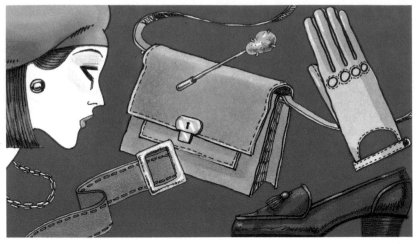

## NATURAL

Minimal, plain, unconstructed styles: silver or gold fine/medium chain necklace, small or medium-scale rounded gold or silver earrings, gold, silver or natural material lapel stickpin, reptile-grain or natural woven leather belts, natural leather shoulder bag or unconstructed pouches, berets, tweed caps, natural straw hats, loafers.

## ROMANTIC

Delicate, intricate ornate styles; antique or baroque dangling earrings, cameo, locket or filigree necklaces, pearl or flower pins, soft leather or crushed suede belts, intricate or bejeweled buckles, small, supple leather or fabric bags with beads, gather or trim, picture hats of lace or horsehair, strappy, slim-heeled open toed shoes or ballet flats.

# ACCESSORIES

## SEASONAL ACCESSORY SUGGESTIONS

### SPRING ACCESSORIES
JEWELRY:
Delicate and light design;
filigree
EYEGLASSES:
Golden brown, ivory, neutral,
metals
SHOES — BELTS — BAGS:
Ivory, camel, tan, navy,
medium brown
METALS:
Gold tones, brass, copper,
enamels — in Palette colors
STONES:
Pearls (cream shade), coral,
jade (apple green), ivory,
moonstone, emerald, topaz

### SUMMER ACCESSORIES
JEWELRY:
Fragile, finely etched;
lightweight and intricate
EYEGLASSES:
Rose, mauve, gray or blue,
neutral, metals
SHOES — BELTS — BAGS:
Light brown, gray, navy,
bone-rose, off-white
METALS:
Silver, rose gold, pewter,
platinum, white gold
STONES:
Rose or blue pearls, opal,
rose ivory, camel, garnet,
amethyst, aquamarine,
rose quartz

### AUTUMN ACCESSORIES
JEWELRY:
Bold designs, wooden pieces,
tortoise shell
EYEGLASSES:
Red-brown or tortoise shell,
neutral, metals
SHOES — BELTS — BAGS:
Brown (dark and light), tan,
bone (camel), gold tones, olive
METALS:
Antique gold, bronze, copper
STONES:
Cream colored pearls,
carnelian, leaf-green jade,
turquoise, cinnabar, agate,
amber, smokey quartz

### WINTER ACCESSORIES
JEWELRY:
Simple designs,
enamels in primary colors
EYEGLASSES:
Blue, burgundy, gray-blue,
or black, neutral or Palette colors,
metals
SHOES — BELTS — BAGS
Black, navy blue, dark brown,
dark gray, white, bone
METALS:
Platinum, silver, chrome,
white gold
STONES:
Pearls (black or white),
white ivory, diamonds/zircon,
emeralds, crystal, sapphire,
lapis lazuli, rubies

The shape of your face can easily be enhanced by any accessory you choose to wear. Together with the right makeup and hairstyle, your accessories are truly the "added attraction". An important fashion accessory is eyewear. The glasses you select can show off the shape of your face and frame it to perfection. Study the illustration below that most resembles your contour and note the helpful hints.

## ROUND

GLASSES:
Select frames that are no wider than your face. Angular frames will de-emphasize roundness. Try wide octagonal or squared frames to create a slimming effect and select a bridge that is wide and somewhat arched. Avoid small styles and any frames that repeat the roundness of your face.
ACCESSORIES:
Long scarfs and necklaces to add more length. Drop-style earrings, moderately long and preferably with straight lines.

## SQUARE

GLASSES:
Choose frames with soft or rounded curves. Try some decorative or contrasting color side bars to draw attention to browline. Avoid square-shaped frames that repeat your structure.
ACCESSORIES:
Medium size round and oval shaped earrings with length and curves are best. Loosely tied scarfs and long necklaces will also soften the angular lines.

## TRIANGULAR

GLASSES:
Broad rimmed frames which are slightly wider than the widest part of the jawline. Lower edges that are narrower and curve upward. Rectangular shapes are good as are aviator and rounded cat's-eye shapes.
ACCESSORIES:
Draw the eye in a vertical direction with the use of scarfs and necklaces. Choose earrings that are above jawline. Avoid dangles and any horizontal pieces at the neckline that will widen the jawline.

# ACCESSORIES

## INVERTED TRIANGLE

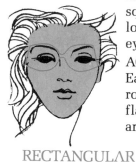

GLASSES:
A combination frame that is round at the top, square at the bottom is best. Aviator, butterfly or low triangle suits your contour well. Avoid cat's-eye shapes.

ACCESSORIES:
Earrings that have some length to them and a round shape rather than sharp angles are most flattering. Scarfs and necklaces with soft curves are good.

## RECTANGULAR

GLASSES:
Oval or aviator shapes are good as long as they create width at the cheekbones. Choose a bridge that is slightly curved. Decorative sidebars will add more width. Avoid rectangular shapes that repeat your face shape.

ACCESSORIES:
Keep all jewelry and scarfs rounded and high at the neck. Earrings that are short and close to the face in rounded or curved shapes will create width through the middle. Avoid dangling earrings.

## OVAL

GLASSES:
Almost any frame design works well provided it does not detract from the oval shape's natural proportion and beauty. Rimless and semi-rimless are especially becoming for the oval. Avoid side-bars, especially low ones which might throw the face off balance.

ACCESSORIES:
A variety of jewelry and scarfs works well for the oval. All shapes are good as long as they are not too extreme.

# 9. MAKEUP

# MAKEUP

The first actor in ancient Greece tied flowers on his face to express his inner self to his audience. Today your inner self still flowers through your face and how you present it to **your** audience. The colors that bloom on your cheeks are just as important as the colors in your wardrobe.

Now that you know about warm and cool skin tones, you can choose your makeup colors without confusion or expensive trial and error. You will pick your way skillfully through the profusion of soft bronzes, clear clarets, and lush peaches at the makeup counter, knowing how to find your exact shades among them. Until now, you may have matched your makeup to your clothes. Now you can match both makeup and clothes to **you.**

Your seasonal color type (warm or cool base) should always be your first consideration whenever selecting any makeup, no matter what your personal style type is.

| SPRING (warm) Make-Up | SUMMER (cool) Make-Up | AUTUMN (warm) Make-Up | WINTER (cool) Make-Up |
|---|---|---|---|
| *Foundation:* | *Foundation:* | *Foundation:* | *Foundation:* |
| Yellow-toned Beige (for light skin) | Rose toned Beige | Yellow-toned Beige (for light skin) | Rose toned Beiges (medium to dark) |
| Gold-toned Beige (for dark skin) | Pink Beige | Copper-toned Beige (for dark skin) | Pink Beige |
| Ivory, Peach (light to dark shades) | Rachel Base | Ivory | Honey Beige |
|  | *Blusher:* | Light to Dark Peach | Rachel Beige |
| *Blusher:* | Light Pink |  | *Blusher:* |
| Peaches | Rose | *Blusher:* | Rosy Red, Blue-Pink |
| Corals | Blue-Pink | Oranges (all) | Burgundy, Plum |
| Peach-Pinks | Light Plum | Gold tones |  |
|  | *Eye Shadow:* | Tawny Peaches | *Eye Shadow:* |
| *Eye Shadow:* | Blue-Gray |  | Lt. Gray/Silver |
| Soft Apricot | Rose/Mauve | *Eye Shadow:* | Lt. Plum/Mauve |
| Green, Aqua | Soft Brown | Green (Olive) | Blue-Gray |
| Soft Brown | Soft Gray | Brown, Copper | Ash Green/Blues |
|  |  | Soft Turquoise |  |
| *Lipsticks:* | *Lipsticks:* |  | *Lipsticks:* |
| Coral, Peach | Pale Pink | *Lipsticks:* | True Red, Blue-Red |
| Warm Peach-Pink | Softened Plum | Peach, Coral | Burgundy, Plum |
| Clear Light Red | Light Burgundy | Orange-Red |  |
|  | Blue-Pink | Brownish-Red |  |

## MAKING UP YOUR FACE

Your face shape determines the correct placement of blusher. Review the six illustrations for fundamental directions in application of color to cheeks, noting the face shape that is closest to yours.

ROUND:

Apply blusher in a sideways V on cheekbones to slim the face. Blend upwards from cheekbone towards temples. Add a touch of blusher to your chin and blend.

**Makeup Goal:**
To minimize and narrow the width and create illusion of length.

SQUARE:

Apply blusher on cheekbones starting at center of eyes. Blend toward temples and apply a dab to forehead and chin.

**Makeup Goal:**
To soften the square angle and reduce the brow and chin areas.

TRIANGULAR:

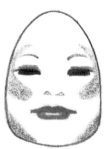

Apply blusher in wide strokes from the hairline to the nose, remaining high on the cheekbones. Soften the jawline with a little blush on both sides.

**Makeup Goal:**
To balance the face by adding width to the forehead and minimizing the jawline.

## INVERTED TRIANGLE:

Apply blusher in a sideways V on cheekbones. Blend upwards from cheekbone to temples extending over the eyebrow to center of forehead. Avoid blusher on chin.

**Makeup Goal:**
To balance the width of your forehead and cheeks with the rest of your face.

## RECTANGULAR:

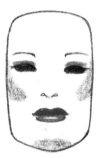

Apply blusher high on cheek bones just below outer corner of eye.
Blend upwards toward temples. Apply a dab of blush at chin and blend to shorten face.

**Makeup Goal:**
To shorten and minimize length and to add width.

## OVAL:

Apply blusher at the most prominent part of your cheekbone and blend upwards to temples.

**Makeup Goal:**
To keep the face in balance and highlight your cheekbones.

# 10. HAIR

## FACING UP TO HAIRSTYLES

The shape, cut and style of your hair should always enhance your face shape as well. Select the face shape that best fits your contour and note suggestions for the complementary hairstyles listed. Remember, a good haircut is the basis of any good hairstyle. The cut should follow the natural flow and lines of your hair while enhancing your facial structure as well.

### ROUND:

Keep fullness above the ears and height at the crown. Keep hair over/around cheek area to minimize fullness. If your hair is worn long it should be fuller at the neck to detract from roundness. Avoid center parts, flat styles, or very full or too short.

**Lengths:**
All lengths will work well as long as hair is fuller at crown.

### SQUARE:

Soften the face with wisps of bangs across forehead. Curls or waves are better than sharp angular styles. Layered cuts and a variety in line works well. Avoid any fullness at the jawline.

**Lengths:**
Longer styles will help lengthen. Especially good if hair falls below the jawline or even longer.

### TRIANGULAR:

Add your width on the top and use full or wispy bangs to widen the forehead area. Irregular lines are good and avoid fullness at jawline. Direct hair closer to cheek and over ears.

**Lengths:**
Short or long will work. For short styles, keep volume and fullness. Longer hair should be at least to neckline, well below jawline.

### INVERTED TRIANGLE:

Soft or loose styles work well. Cover part of your forehead to make it appear narrower and consider bangs. Fullness at the jawline or shoulders will add width. Avoid low side parts and severe tailored styles.

**Lengths:**
Shoulder lengths work well and the shortest styles should fall to the chin or below.

**RECTANGULAR:**
Hair should be full at the sides, minimum height at top. Bangs are good to cut illusion of length. A side part is better than a center one. Avoid pulling hair straight back or close to the head.
**Lengths:** Mid length is best.

**OVAL:**
Styles that frame your face are the most flattering. Keep the look uncomplicated and soft so as not to detract from your ideal shape.
**Lengths:** Any length as long as it maintains your natural balance.

Haircolor products are divided into four categories.

**Temporary** color stays on hair until shampooed out, approximately 1 or 2 shampoos. It is a good method for individuals who do not want permanent color.

**Semi-Permanent** color lasts until it wears off or is shampooed out (4-6 shampoos). It is a great way to cover gray without changing your natural color.

**Permanent** color lasts until it grows out. It offers the most dramatic change, allowing you to go lighter, darker, cover gray or enhance your natural color.

**Highlighting or Frosting** color is permanent, needing about four touch-ups a year. This process is good for adding tone to the hair and providing blonde highlights.

## HOW TO CHOOSE HAIRCOLOR

Here is a breakdown of color choices apropriate for each seasonal type:

| SPRING | SUMMER | AUTUMN | WINTER |
|---|---|---|---|
| **Hair Colors** | **Hair Colors** | **Hair Colors** | **Hair Colors** |
| Warm, golden or reddish tones. | Cool, ashen tones | Warm, Red highlights, Auburn, Golden Brown | Cool, ashen tones |
| Yellow-Blonde | Ash Blonde | Tones | Ash Brown, Ash Blonde |
| Golden Blonde | Ash Brunette | Golden Blonde | Blue-Black |
| Golden Brown | Gray: natural or highlight | Golden Brown | Gray: natural or highlighted |
| Red Brown | with a rinse for highlighting | Red Brown | Frosting or light streaking |
| Strawberry | Frosting or light streaking | Red, Strawberry | in ash tones only |
| Red or Golden Henna | in ash tones only | Red Henna | Avoid red tones |
| Avoid partial Gray, | Avoid red tones | Best to cover gray | |
| Avoid Frosting | | Avoid frosting | |

Now that you know the spectacular difference color can make in your life, why don't you think about coloring your hair?

# 11. FRAGRANCES

## CHOOSING YOUR SIGNATURE FRAGRANCE

No matter what your season or personality type, you are free to choose any scent that strongly appeals to you — and to those you want to please. Don't feel locked in by any "rules" on fragrances. If you still haven't found your signature fragrance, here are some suggestions about where to start looking.

SPRING — Light, fresh florals or fruits, "greens" and citrus scents.

SUMMER — Single florals or floral bouquets.

AUTUMN — Blends of fruity fragrances, musks, woodland scents, and spices.

WINTER — Sophisticated scents; spicy, exotic scents, oriental blends.

CLASSIC — Subtle, traditional.    DRAMATIC — Exotic, oriental.

NATURAL — Fresh, floral.    ROMANTIC — Flowery, soft.

# DISCOVER YOUR PERSONAL STYLE

To receive your FREE Style Analysis with the purchase of your Personal Style Kit, complete the easy questions below.

## YOUR PERSONAL STYLE ANALYSIS QUESTIONNAIRE

Please read every question carefully and check the answer that best describes you. Since this is a very personalized analysis, it's important that you answer **all** questions.

In order to answer all questions accurately, you'll need these items:

- A full length mirror
- Pencil and paper
- Hair pulled back away from face
- If possible, a friend or family member to help you (it's often difficult to be objective about oneself)

If you have 1 or 2 color photos of yourself in natural daylight (i.e. Polaroid), include them with your completed questionnaire. All photos will be returned to you promptly with your style anlaysis.

---

1. My Personal Style type (as learned in Chapter 1) is:
   - A ☐ CLASSIC (also known as: Elegant, Traditional, Tailored, Conservative, Sophisticated, Formal)
   - B ☐ DRAMATIC (also known as: Glamorous, Exotic, Creative, Theatrical, Artistic, Sexy)
   - C ☐ NATURAL (also known as: Casual, Sporty, Informal, Country, Outdoorsy, Basic)
   - D ☐ ROMANTIC (also known as: (Feminine, Ingenue, Soft, Victorian, Delicate, Poetic)

2. The selection that best describes my personality is:
   - A ☐ Soft, charming and supportive
   - B ☐ Free-spirited, energetic, friendly
   - C ☐ Understated, practical, poised
   - D ☐ Independent, stimulating, flamboyant

3. The woman whose personal style I most admire is:
   - A ☐ Cher
   - B ☐ Goldie Hawn
   - C ☐ Jackie (Kennedy) Onassis
   - D ☐ Jane Seymour

4. The selection that best describes my clothing preference is:
   - A ☐ Comfortable/loose
   - B ☐ Tailored/fitted
   - C ☐ Architectural/contrasted
   - D ☐ Detailed/frilly

5. The selection that best describes my preference in line design is:
   - A ☐ Sharp/angular
   - B ☐ Swirled/curled
   - C ☐ Solid/straight
   - D ☐ Waved/watered

6. The selection that best describes my fabric preference is:
   - A ☐ Soft, drapey, flowing
   - B ☐ Easy-care, natural
   - C ☐ Shiny, ornate, unusual
   - D ☐ Woven, smooth, matte-finish

7. My lifework (as discussed in chapter 2) is:
   - A ☐ Student
   - B ☐ Working Single
   - C ☐ Homemaker/Single
   - D ☐ Working mother
   - E ☐ Work in office
   - F ☐ Work at home
   - G ☐ Work as a volunteer
   - H ☐ Other _____

8. My age group is:
   - A ☐ Under 25
   - B ☐ 25-35
   - C ☐ 36-45
   - D ☐ 46-55
   - E ☐ 56 and over

9. Other than for work, I dress up for special occasions each week approximately:
   - A ☐ once a week
   - B ☐ twice weekly
   - C ☐ three times weekly
   - D ☐ four-five times
   - E ☐ five or more times
   - F ☐ None or seldom

If you wish to retain this page, please send a photocopy of same.

10. My body type (as learned in Chapter 3) is best described as:
    A ☐ Hourglass
    B ☐ Triangle
    C ☐ Inverted Triangle
    D ☐ Rectangle

11. My face shape (as learned in Chapter 4) is best described as:
    A ☐ Round
    B ☐ Square
    C ☐ Triangular
    D ☐ Inverted Triangle
    E ☐ Rectangle
    F ☐ Oval

12. The selection that best describes my favorite colors is:
    A ☐ Pastels and tints
    B ☐ Neutrals and muted
    C ☐ Subdued and earthy
    D ☐ Bold and contrasting

13. My Seasonal Color type (as learned in Chapter 5) is:
    A ☐ Spring (warm colors)
    B ☐ Summer (cool colors)
    C ☐ Autumn (warm colors)
    D ☐ Winter (cool colors)
    E ☐ Unknown

14. The selection that best describes my makeup preference is:
    A ☐ Vivid
    B ☐ Polished
    C ☐ Delicate
    D ☐ Minimal

15. The selection that best describes my hairstyle preference is:
    A ☐ Carefree or straight
    B ☐ Timeless and neat
    C ☐ Soft curls or feathered
    D ☐ Geometric or striking

16. The selection that best describes my fragrance preference is:
    A ☐ Floral
    B ☐ Woodsy
    C ☐ Oriental
    D ☐ Spicy

17. Additional comments on my characteristics

_____

_____

_____

_____

_____

# FREE STYLE ANALYSIS
## with your purchase of a Revelli Personal Style Kit

See order form on page 94 for cost (C & D)

# DISCOVER YOUR BEST COLORS

## To receive your FREE Color Analysis with the purchase of your seasonal color kit, complete the easy questions below.

### YOUR PERSONAL COLOR ANALYSIS QUESTIONNAIRE

Please read every question carefully and check the answer that best describes you. Since this is a very personalized analysis, it's important that you answer all questions. Take special care when answering questions about skin tone since your season is based primarily on your skin tone.

In order to answer the questions accurately, you'll need these items:

- natural daylight (not fluorescent light)
- a sheet of 8½ × 11" white paper
- a mirror large enough to reflect your face and hair
- a family member or friend to help you (it's often difficult to be objective about oneself)

If you have 1 or 2 color photos (i.e. Polaroid), of yourself in natural daylight include them with your completed questionnaire. All photos will be returned to you promptly with your color anlaysis.

---

## SKIN COLOR

Your skin will fall into one of the following categories: very fair, light, medium or dark. It may also have a specific tint such as pink, peach or yellow. In each of the questions below check the answers that describes your skin as closely as possible.

For question 1, hold your forearm over the white paper with the inner side of your wrist facing up. This is the best area for determining your natural skin tone.

1. **How would you best describe your skin tone?**
   - A ☐ Olive (light, medium, dark), black
   - B ☐ Light beige with a pink tinge
   - C ☐ Rosy pink, deep pink
   - D ☐ Red rose-beige, gray beige
   - E ☐ Ivory
   - F ☐ Peach, peach-beige, peach-pink
   - G ☐ Golden beige, coppery beige, golden black, tawny

2. **What is your basic skin color?**
   - A ☐ Very fair
   - B ☐ Light
   - C ☐ Medium
   - D ☐ Dark

3. **Do you have a sallow (yellowish) cast to your skin?**
   - A ☐ Yes          B ☐ No

4. **When I tan my skin turns:**
   - A ☐ Golden brown
   - B ☐ Red
   - C ☐ Bronze or copper brown
   - D ☐ Berry brown (dark brown)

## HAIR COLOR

5. **What color was your hair when you were 9 or 10 years old?**
   - A ☐ White blond (towhead)
   - B ☐ Ash blond
   - C ☐ Yellow or golden blond
   - C ☐ Light brown
   - E ☐ Medium brown
   - F ☐ Dark brown
   - G ☐ Red or auburn
   - H ☐ Black

6. **How would you best describe your natural hair color today?**
   - A ☐ Blue-black or brown (med. to dark)
   - B ☐ Ash or smoky blond
   - C ☐ Smoky brown
   - D ☐ Platinum (no golden highlights)
   - E ☐ Blue-gray
   - F ☐ Red, chestnut, auburn, golden honey-blond, golden honey-brown, copper brown
   - G ☐ Yellow-blond, strawberry-blond, golden brown, blond-red, golden gray
   - H ☐ Salt and pepper, silver-gray, white (snow)

7. **The color of my hair when I look in the mirror today is:**
   - A ☐ Light    B ☐ Medium    C ☐ Dark

8. **What color are the natural highlights (sheen) in your hair today?**
   - A ☐ Ash blond          D ☐ Golden yellow
   - B ☐ Red                E ☐ Gray
   - C ☐ Blue-black         F ☐ None

9. **Do you color your hair?**
   - A ☐ Yes          B ☐ No

If you wish to retain these questionnaire pages, please send a photocopy of same.

## EYE COLOR

10. My eye color is:     A ☐ Light     B ☐ Medium     C ☐ Dark

11. Which color best describes your eyes?
    A ☐ Blue     B ☐ Green     C ☐ Aqua     D ☐ Gray-blue     E ☐ Hazel     F ☐ Gray
    G ☐ Brown     H ☐ Black

12. Do your eyes change color depending on what you're wearing?     A ☐ Yes     B ☐ No

13. Which group of colors do you like the best?
    (Make your selection based on the group of colors, not on an individual color.)
    A ☐ Pure white, pure black, charcoal gray, true red, royal blue, burgundy, dark navy
    B ☐ Soft white, rose brown, pearl gray, mauve, pastel blue, soft lavender
    C ☐ Oyster white, dark brown, rust, olive green, teal blue, gold, camel
    D ☐ Peach, ivory, turquoise, apricot, golden brown, bright clear yellow, medium blue,
         clear yellow green

14. What intensity of colors do you prefer?
    A ☐ Soft pastels or tints     B ☐ Bold, strong and primary     C ☐ Clear, vivid and warm
    D ☐ Muted, earthy, naturals

15. My family heritage is:     A ☐ _____
                               B ☐ I am unsure of my family origins

16. I have been color analyzed and my season is: _____

17. Additional comments on my characteristics: _____

---

# FREE COLOR ANALYSIS
## with your purchase of a REVELLI SEASONAL COLOR KIT

# REVELLI ORDER FORM

My Seasonal Color group is:   (Please circle one)
SPRING            SUMMER            AUTUMN            WINTER            UNKNOWN

My Personal Style type is:   (Please circle one)
CLASSIC            DRAMATIC            NATURAL            ROMANTIC            UNKNOWN

☐ I am enclosing the style ☐  color ☐   Questionnaire(s) on pgs. 90–93.
☐ Please send me the items checked on the Revelli order form below.

## REVELLI ORDER FORM

A ☐ COLOR ANALYSIS QUESTIONNAIRE — **FREE** (with the purchase of a Revelli Color Kit) for anyone unsure of their seasonal color type. See COLOR KIT (B) below.

B ☐ COLOR KIT — Wallet size Revelli Personal Palette with fabric swatches in your best colors, tips on how to wear your colors in wardrobe, accessories, makeup; and a national brands haircolor shades and cosmetics list in your best colors (circle season above or refer to "A") . . . . . . . . . . . . . . . . . . . . . . . . . . . $21.00

C ☐ STYLE ANALYSIS QUESTIONNAIRE — **FREE** (with the purchase of a Revelli Style Kit) for anyone unsure of their personal style type. See STYLE KIT (D) below.

D ☐ STYLE KIT — Your individual wardrobe plan featuring clothing illustrations designed for your personality, lifestyle and body type. Includes tips on what clothes and accessories suit your personal style plus additional tips on how to create your own INDIVIDUAL statement (circle style type above or refer to "C") . . . . . . . . . . . . . . . . . . . . . . . . . . . . . . . . . . . . . . . . . . . . . . . . . . . $21.00

E ☐ NEWSLETTER — "MAKING NEWS", Revelli's colorful quarterly forecast on fashion, beauty, and more . . . . . . . . . . . . . . . . . . . . . . . . . . . . . . . . . .$16.00

F ☐ VIDEO — This visually exciting COLOR AND YOU (VHS-45 mins.) comes with a 32-page color booklet and features Clare Revelli with tips on makeup, haircolor, scarfs, jewelry, belts, hosiery, eyewear and more . . . . . . . . . . . . . . . . . . $23.50

G ☐ BOOK — Clare Revelli's best-selling COLOR AND YOU, A Guide To Discovering Your Best Colors — for men and women . . . . . . . . . . . . . . . . . . . . . . . . . . $7.50

H ☐ BOOK — Clare Revelli's best-selling STYLE & YOU, Every Woman's Guide To Total Style . . . . . . . . . . . . . . . . . . . . . . . . . . . . . . . . . . . . . . . . . . . . . . $7.50

I ☐ BOOK — THE COLORS OF YOUR LIFE with Clairol and Clare Revelli. The definitive full-color seasonal haircolor book includes a complimentary skintone analyzer, makeup lists, national brand haircolor shades by season, color palettes and more! . . . . . . . . . . . . . . . . . . . . . . . . . . . . . . . . . . . . . . . . . . . . . . . . . . $10.00

J ☐ PALETTE CARDS — A seasonal color card for each of the four seasons, 20 colors per card plus makeup suggestions. Set of Four . . . . . . . . . . . . . . . . . . . . . $5.00

| | | |
|---|---|---|
| Sub-total | | _____ |
| CA residents add sales tax | | _____ |
| Total amount enclosed | | _____ |

All above prices include postage and handling. Discounts available with larger quantity orders.
(Write or Call Revelli for information: 415-673-6313)